The Standard Bearer

by
David Raynor

The Standard Bearer

A BIOGRAPHY OF CHARLES OXLEY

BY

DAVID RAYNOR

2001
Quinta Press

Quinta Press

Meadow View, Weston Rhyn, Oswestry, Shropshire,
England, SY10 7RN
Visit our web-site: www.quintapress.com

ISBN 1 897856 11 3

Copyright © 2001 by David Raynor

First published 2001

Reprinted 2002, 2003, 2012

CONTENTS

Contents v
Foreword by John C Beyer of mediawatch–uk vii
Preface xi
Acknowledgements xii
1 Family, Fire-fighting and Faith 1
2 Snapshots from Schooldays 13
3 Teaching, Marriage and Tower College 23
4 School Philosophy and Scarisbrick Hall 38
5 Battles with Broadcasters 52
6 Sex Shops and Blasphemy 64
7 Punish the Wicked, Care for the Victims 76
8 Religious Education and Riots 90
9 Spy among the Paedophiles 104
10 Needs of North India 116
11 School Number Three in Scotland 126
12 Dismay at Declining Standards 141
13 Final Battles 155

FOREWORD

A MUCH VALUED MENTOR

Charles Oxley was an impressive man not only in stature but also in manner—and we know that 'manners maketh the man'!

He always struck me as being humble and self-effacing and yet he had the confidence and determination to see that right should always prevail. He was dedicated to his vocation as a teacher and headmaster and he always had the well being of his students at heart. He was concerned that they should have the best education and go on to enter wider society as mature and responsible young citizens.

These concerns led him into dangerous territory beyond his first calling because he had the wisdom to understand that the pupils, and young people in general, were being subjected to conflicting influences outside the school environment.

As I recall he first contacted Mary Whitehouse, and the National Viewers' and Listeners' Association (now called mediawatch-uk), when he sent us some of the correspondence he had had with officials at the BBC. This led to an invitation to Mary to address Scarisbrick Hall School. So impressed was she that Charles was soon invited to serve on the Association's Executive Committee where he often enthralled us as he relived his exploits. There he became a friend and a much-valued mentor in the campaign we were waging against bad taste and indecency on television.

In this book it is evident that Charles exercised great patience and fortitude in his writing as in his life. This was characteristic. He was brave and courageous in exposing corruption and immorality and his attempts to disrupt organised paedophile activity put him at considerable risk. His campaign against swearing and blasphemy on television won the support of eminent people in politics and in the media itself. He was a very thoughtful man and had a clear understanding of what it means to be a Christian activist in a hostile world. Charles Oxley sacrificed much and in persevering set us all an example.

This book gives testimony to a man who, above all, loved God and loved his neighbour in the broadest sense and to this day he leaves a gap in the ranks of those still fighting the good fight.

JOHN C BEYER,
Director of mediawatch–uk
June 2001
Ashford, Kent

mediawatch–uk can be contacted at:
3 Willow House, Kennington Road, Ashford, Kent. TN24 0NR
Tel: (01233) 633936
Fax: (01233) 633836

PREFACE

It is thirteen years since Charles Oxley died, but for decades prior to that day in 1987 he had foreseen and fought against the erosion of moral standards in Britain. Not for him the fatalistic shrug of the shoulders; he stood when others took their ease, spoke out when the majority remained silent, took firm action when many just wrung their hands in despair.

After his death, his wife Muriel kindly allowed me free access into his study and his files to discover aspects of the man that I had only heard about. My interest in him, fostered by nineteen years in his employment, became a fascination, something I wanted others to share. Hence this book. He evidently had thoughts of writing his own life story, because I found the draft of one chapter among his papers; I have unashamedly included it, with only minimal alteration, as chapter 2 of this biography.

Among his papers I also found a series of loose-leaf sheets, presumably the outline of another book he hoped one day to write. Each sheet was headed with a question from the Bible, asked by Jesus or another character. Charles' note on the cover sheet expressed his intention to add a half-page comment on each question. One page was headed with this double question from Psalm 94 v 16: *Who will rise up for me against the evil-doers? Who will stand up for me against the workers of iniquity?* Nothing could better express the motivation for much of Charles Oxley's life and work.

He saw everything in black-and-white, good-and-evil terms. He probably never heard the term 'political correctness', but it is something he would have despised nonetheless, as it would, to him, have summed up the removal of important benchmarks. After all, the Jesus whom he served and followed spoke about divisions between sheep and goats, light and darkness, the foolish and the faithful. Inevitably also, some individuals who were strongly with him on certain issues, were equally strongly against him on others. It is a mark of maturity to be able to disagree without being disagreeable.

In pioneering three independent schools, where the Christian faith mattered at least as much as high academic standards, Charles put his beliefs into action. Likewise, in his crusades, campaigns and committees—at one time, he told me, he was involved with thirty-six causes—he held the standard aloft tirelessly. One of the hundreds of letters received by Muriel after his death aptly summed him up in comparing Charles Oxley to Mr Valiant-for-Truth in Bunyan's *Pilgrim's Progress*.

ACKNOWLEDGEMENTS

I wish to express my gratitude to the family of the late Charles Oxley, particularly his late wife Muriel and their daughter Rachel, the Principal of Tower College, Rainhill, Merseyside, for access to his papers and for photographs kindly lent. I am indebted to the *Liverpool Daily Post and Echo* for permission to use the photograph of the aftermath of the Toxteth riots. I am also indebted to Mrs Joan Molyneux, a secretary at Tower College, for volunteering to type the first draft of the book; and to Dr Digby James for his assistance in publishing the book.

Chapter 1

FAMILY, FIRE-FIGHTING AND FAITH

Charles Alexander Oxley was born on 25th February 1922 in a house in Randolph Gardens, Partick, an area of Glasgow. He had strong Scottish ancestry on his mother's side, but his father's family came from the Lancashire industrial town of St Helens, where Charles grew up and lived for most of his life. Many people associate St Helens with either glass-making (Pilkington's have been major employers for generations) or Rugby League, and it was in another town famous for its Rugby League team—Warrington—that Charles' paternal grandfather, C.B. Oxley, first found employment. It was in the coal mines that Charles Benoni Oxley began his working life; in later years he changed the 'Benoni' to Benjamin, but it mattered little, since everybody knew him as 'C.B.'

From the mines he moved to a drapery stall on Warrington market, where he found keen competition, particularly in the main part of his business, which was ladies' aprons. He decided that the most economical way of running the business was to make the aprons himself, and it says much for his energy and business acumen that he eventually opened a large department store in the centre of St

Helens, a few miles away. We may need to look no further than C.B. to find the source of his more illustrious grandson's business skills and capacity for hard work.

C.B. Oxley had a deep and lifelong Christian faith, which led him into membership of what used to be called the Plymouth Brethren. The Brethren movement had divided in the late 1840s: the 'Open' Brethren, led by George Müller, separated from the 'Exclusive' Brethren, led by J.N. Darby, because the latter excluded from membership those who did not hold to what they considered to be sound doctrine. The 'Open' Brethren had no central organisation, their assemblies being independent of each other and led by their own local overseers; their communion service, or breaking of bread, was open to all true believers. Sadly, though, the words of Dr Griffiths Thomas have proved to be all too accurate: 'The Brethren are remarkable people for rightly dividing the Word of Truth and wrongly dividing themselves.' In the late 1880s some of the 'Open' Brethren felt that the movement's magazine, *The Witness*, had become too dogmatic and started an alternative, *Needed Truth*, to stimulate interest in Bible teaching on a wider front.

By 1894, the 'Needed Truth' assemblies had separated from the 'Open' Brethren and given themselves the title 'Churches of God'. It was in this stream of the Brethren movement that C.B. Oxley worshipped and served God. Those within the assemblies recognised his deep spirituality and appointed him an overseer and later a 'leading brother'. He had musical talent and a gift for hymn-writing, several of his compositions being published in Brethren song-books and two of them—*Come let us sing this song of love* and *From the cross unto glory*—remaining favourites to this day.

In 1895, at the age of 29, C.B. married a 35-year-old widow, Mary Ann McGinn, and in the following year David Charlton Oxley, Charles' father, was born. Mary seems to have been a meek and unassuming woman who doted on her son.

Charles' maternal grandfather also came from humble beginnings. Alexander McGaw started life as a grocer's boy and later opened his own grocery business in Drummore, Wigtown. He too was a devout man of God, with a deep understanding of biblical truth and a powerful gift of oratory in expounding it. Alexander married Nellie Sterling, whose family had a coach-building business and considerable musical talents. When they first married, they lived in rooms in Chapel Street, Hamilton, before moving to the pleasant seaside town of Drummore on the Mull of Galloway in the far south-west of Scotland. Their next move brought them to the house in Partick where grandson Charles would be born. Both their daughters, Maggie and Jeannie, had musical skills and Charles was to inherit some of them from Maggie, his mother.

Margaret McGaw was born in Hamilton and lived long enough to see Charles establish his third independent school in that town. His first school was situated near St Helens, the town to which Margaret moved after marrying David Charlton Oxley in 1919. David was now well established in his father C.B.'s department store and he and Margaret made their home in Dunriding Lane. Their first child, David junior, was born in 1920, a quiet, gentle, rather nervous boy, very special to both sides of the family as the first grandchild of the Oxleys and the McGaws. When his parents' marriage broke up it was David, aged 18, who took responsibility for his mother's wellbeing. He himself then became ill with a lengthy and debilitating condition from which he eventually died at the age of only 29.

Charles Alexander Oxley was the second child. Known throughout his life to family and close friends as Charlie, he was much more robust than David. One who knew him as a child recalls 'a very good-looking little boy, but full of mischief.'

Fifteen months younger than Charlie was Helen Margaret, the only daughter and an attractive child in every way. When Helen was 15, her parents separated and Margaret took the four children to live in Glasgow. Helen took a secretarial course, then worked in a bank before becoming personal secretary to Mr McDonald of the McDonald Biscuit Company. In 1953 she married Samuel Chesney from Belfast and went to live in that city. Samuel's widowed father lived with them and in time Helen's mother Margaret moved there as well. Helen and Samuel had one son, David Sterling Chesney.

Then tragedy struck. Samuel was preparing to start a garage business and as he worked to remove part of an upstairs floor of the premises, he fell down and the ceiling crashed on him. He was killed instantly. His death was a severe blow to Helen, but her distress was increased by the fact that Irish inheritance laws made no allowance for the widow. It says much for her resourcefulness and determination that she secured a job with the Milk Marketing Board, enabling her to maintain the home. The shock of Samuel's death traumatised Margaret, who became ill and was unable to do much to help around the house.

Further tragedy was to follow. Helen, Margaret and little David crossed the Irish Sea by ferry to pay a visit to Charlie and his family in St Helens. During the crossing David must have caught a virus, so on arrival in St Helens they called a doctor. He told them it was indeed a virus but he failed to disclose that it was in fact polio. He assured Helen that David would be all right, but within a short time of their return to Belfast, Helen herself became very ill and was diagnosed as having polio. A fortnight later she died, leaving a young son and an invalid mother.

By now Charlie was married to Muriel and they took responsibility for giving Margaret and David a home and ensuring David had a good education. In Margaret's will, made out in 1981, she paid tribute to her son and daughter-in-law: 'I wish to record my grateful thanks to Charlie and Muriel for the beautiful home fitted up in every essential and comfort for David and me on our having to leave Ireland. In particular, the thoughtful mother care by Muriel for David from early childhood, and for me even to old age continued most generously.'

The fourth child of David and Margaret Oxley was John Alistair, the only one of the children not to share the family's Christian faith. He was probably the one most affected by his parents' marital break-up. Then, at the age of 11, he was evacuated from Glasgow

Charles (back, centre) with sister Helen and brothers David (right) and John (front).

because of the blitz to go and live with his grandparents in Ayr. Although he was undoubtedly clever, he did not see the need for disciplined study in his younger days. For a time before his marriage he lived with Charlie and Muriel; the last contact the family had was from an address in the south of England.

The home which David and Margaret set up in Dunriding Lane, St Helens, was comfortable but not extravagant. Family life was orderly, with firm discipline, but there was plenty of fun as well. The success of the department store enabled them to employ maids, but the children were certainly not spoilt. Life revolved very much around their church activities—the main Sunday meetings, Sunday School, bible studies, weekend conferences—and their friends were therefore mainly from Christian circles. One family in particular—the Cholertons—were very close, spiritually, socially and geographically: not only were they fellow-members of the Assembly Hall Church of God, but they lived only a hundred yards or so from the Oxley family home.

The Cholertons had six children. Nora, the second eldest, was a close friend of Helen Oxley during the years in St Helens and also when the Oxley children moved with their mother to Glasgow. The Oxley boys were good pals of Eddie and Reggie, numbers three and four of the Cholerton clan. Muriel was next to youngest and although three-year-old Charlie Oxley first set eyes on her when she was taken to the church meeting at two or three weeks old, there was no special friendship between them until she was twenty.

Charles' parents, David and Maggie (at a time when a fox fur was an acceptable accessory!).

Charlie's father, David, is remembered as a handsome man, often to be seen with a Bible in his hand. He sought to train his family in Christian ways and, like C.B. before him, was highly respected in the church. It was therefore a shattering blow to both David and his father when David's marriage broke up. Church life as well as family life suffered, for the sanctity of marriage has always held a central position in Brethren teaching on family life. The reasons for the split remain a mystery, as there was no sign of domestic unrest to those who knew the family. Nevertheless, Margaret decided to take the children north to Glasgow while David and C.B. both felt obliged to withdraw from membership of their church assembly. Ten years later David re-married and went to live in Tasmania for the last twenty-three years of his life. He died in that faraway place in 1975.

When Charles' theology became formulated in young adulthood, he could not justify from the Scriptures the re-marriage of a divorcee. He had been brought up to accept totally the authority of the Bible in matters of faith and doctrine, and to him the words of Jesus were clear, categorical and uncompromising: 'Whosoever shall put away his wife except for adultery and shall marry another, committeth adultery: and whoso marrieth her which is put away doth commit adultery.' (Matthew 19 verse 9 in the Authorised or King James Version of the Bible, much preferred by many Brethren including Charles Oxley.) He held firmly to that fundamentalist position throughout his life and was not slow to defend it when he saw the danger of it being eroded. In the late 1970s and early 1980s, for example, the Church of England was debating the re-marriage of divorcees on church premises and also whether a divorcee could be ordained into the ministry of the church. Charles used the correspondence columns of *The Church Times* and *The Church of England Newspaper* to engage in the debate.

> According to my understanding of Christian teaching on marriage, a man whose wife deserts him... is not free to re-marry during the lifetime of that partner. One cannot promise *till death us do part* to two living persons.

> Jesus taught that marriage vows were sacred and inviolable, and that a 'marriage' to a second woman or man is an adulterous relationship. I believe the exceptive phrase 'except for adultery' refers to cases where, because of previous undisclosed fornication, the marriage was invalid.

When He said, 'the two shall become one,' he could not have put it more strongly.

When a Church of England bishop was praised as being 'enlightened' for speaking in favour of the ordination of divorcees, Charles asked:—

Enlightened? By whose light? It cannot be by the light of Him who claimed to be the Light of the World, for He re-affirmed the inviolability of marriage with the words, 'What therefore God hath joined together, let not man put asunder.'

How can a person, who has broken his own marriage vows, charge another person with the solemn vows of Holy Matrimony and warn of his having to 'answer at the dreadful day of judgement'? It makes a mockery of marriage.

How can a person who before God has vowed 'to have and to hold from this day forward, for better or worse... till death us do part, according to God's holy ordinance', break such cast-iron promises and then have the nerve to come back and ask to make the same cast-iron promises to someone else? I repeat, it makes a mockery of marriage.

Put the two together—a divorced minister/priest charging a divorced man and/or woman in a 're-marriage' service, to 'live together after God's ordinance in the holy estate of matrimony'—and you have the height of hypocrisy.

As with so many of Charles Oxley's moral judgements, grey areas were hard to find, but in this matter he wrote and spoke not only on the authority of the Bible but also from personal experience of the damage caused by breaking God's laws. The break-up of his parents' marriage may have left a deeper scar on his mother and brothers and sister than on himself, but in his schoolmastering he came across all too many children who had been emotionally damaged by divorce.

In a letter to the *Liverpool Daily Post* in December 1979 he traced the pathway to easier divorce over the previous thirteen years:—

It was the Archbishop's Commission on marriage and divorce which published a report (*Putting Asunder*, SPCK, 1966) that formed the basis of the Divorce Reform Act 1969. The Archbishop's Commission recommended that divorce should be allowed where a marriage could be shown to have irretrievably broken down. These were new and unscriptural grounds for divorce.

They caused many people to believe the Church of England had come to accept divorce and 're-marriage' as legitimate and it was to try and resolve this confusion that a further Commission (*Marriage, Divorce and the Church*, 1971) recommended that the 're-marriage' of divorced persons in church should be allowed.

In the main, this has been resisted, but the Church of England has been seen to lower its standards. It is largely in consequence of the Church's failure to stand firmly on this and other moral issues, that it is fast losing its moral influence in western society.

In these permissive days, the clear and uncompromising teaching of Jesus on this subject is thought to be harsh and unrealistic. But the breaking of the marriage vows causes very harsh and very real suffering, especially to children.

The break-up of the marriage of David and Margaret Oxley occurred when Charlie was 16 years old. He had left school at 15 to work in the family business, and when his mother took the family to Glasgow, he found employment at Gardners', a high-class furniture store in that city. The young man he replaced there was one David Ferguson, also a keen Christian. When David went to work for another company he kept in touch with the workforce at Gardners', especially when he learnt that the new young employee was maintaining a strong witness to the Christian faith. He never met Charlie during those years but followed his career with interest and admiration; his long-cherished wish to meet him was fulfilled when he attended a Prize Day at Hamilton College in 1986. Charles' third school was then just three years old and David had every reason to be thrilled by what his young replacement at the furniture store had achieved in the intervening years.

At the outbreak of the Second World War Charlie Oxley saw clearly, at the age of 17, what his own principles required of him. Even though he hated what Hitler and the Nazis were doing, he could not personally take part in military action if it meant killing innocent individual Germans. Accordingly he became a conscientious objector, went before an official tribunal to argue his position and, instead of joining the military fighters, he enrolled with the fire fighters. Glasgow was a major target of the blitz, so that men in the Fire Service enjoyed no soft option during the war.

Family, Fire-Fighting and Faith

Charles during his war service with the Fire Brigade at Haddington, Glasgow

One night when German planes were attacking several targets in the west of Scotland, the alarm bell sounded for action. The crew quickly assembled, only to find they were one man short. Delay could cost lives, so immediately—and typically—Charlie took the vacant place in the crew.

Modern fire engines have much safer seating arrangements for their crews, but in the 1940s, apart from two or three men in the cab, the crew went out perched on ledges, clinging precariously to the outside of the machine. Being a late stand-in for this emergency, Charlie was still buttoning up his tunic as the engine hurtled through the city and a sudden change of direction threw him to the ground. He was badly injured and they rushed him to the nearest hospital in a critical condition. Although he eventually made a good recovery, there were times throughout his life when pains in the neck and back brought back the horror of that wartime accident.

He had been due to preach the following Sunday at the Brethren assembly in Olive Hall, Partick. Whenever he had a preaching appointment, it was his custom to ask God each day beforehand for someone to be saved at that meeting. Though he could no longer fulfil the appointment, it seems that his prayers were not wasted but rather re-directed by God: during the weeks of recovery in hospital he had many spiritual conversations with men in his ward and to his great delight one of them became a Christian.

To witness a person finding faith in Christ, or being 'born again' in biblical language, remained one of life's treasured privileges for Charles Oxley. In all his campaigning and crusading to try and establish his vision of godly standards in society, he recognised that society is made up of individuals and that each individual needed to make a personal commitment of faith in Jesus Christ. If a man was truly born again by the Holy Spirit, his attitudes would change, his life would be transformed in no small measure, his moral standards would certainly improve and society would be enriched.

Charlie had been brought up to attend three services every Sunday with his brothers and sister. Their father served not only as an overseer in the assembly but also as superintendent of the Sunday School. The young Oxleys were happy enough to go along to the meetings, although Charlie is known to have found Sunday School 'rather a bore', a judgement which he probably never shared with his father! The children had to memorise dozens of Scripture verses, especially those relating to the doctrine of salvation by grace through faith in Christ. Assembly members, including the children, would talk as readily about salvation, faith, being born again and everlasting life as others today would speak about the weather or television soaps. Charlie could not remember a time when he did not believe that Jesus was the Son of God and died to pay the penalty for the sin of the whole human race. If anyone happened to ask him whether he was saved—and the question was by no means rare in those days and in those circles—he always replied that he was.

In June 1930, when his older brother David asked to be baptised, 8-year-old Charlie also applied and was accepted. Baptism among the Brethren had nothing to do with sprinkling a few drops of water on a baby's head, as they could find no scriptural evidence for such a performance. Baptism meant total immersion of a Christian believer; it demonstrated that person's identification with the death and resurrection of Jesus Christ by symbolically burying the old life under the water and rising up as a 'new creation'. Even as an 8-year-old,

Charlie understood the meaning and importance of taking his stand in this way as a follower of Jesus.

One thing bothered him, though: often, in meetings of the assembly, people would speak of their experience of conversion and could specify the day and even the moment when it had happened. Charlie could not be so precise about his own salvation and therefore wondered whether he really was saved at all.

Such concerns still affected his thinking a couple of years later when he was particularly struck by teaching on the second coming of Jesus and the biblical references to believers being 'caught up to meet the Lord in the air.' One late afternoon that winter, he arrived home from school to find nobody in. This was most unusual. The big old house at the corner of Dunriding Lane and St George's Road in St Helens, wrapped in the dullness of a wintry evening and unexpectedly deserted, struck young Charlie as distinctly eerie. Then the awful truth dawned: the Lord must have returned, the rest of the family had been caught up to meet Him and he himself—well, he couldn't have been saved after all. He was the only one of the family left behind! He rushed frantically from room to room, desperate to find someone yet trying to convince himself that everything was all right. Never was a young lad so relieved to see his family again a few minutes later.

Not long after that scare Charlie was fully assured of his salvation. It dawned on him that some of the Scripture verses he had had to memorise were promises of God:—

> John 5 v 24 : He that heareth my word and believeth on him that sent me hath everlasting life and shall not come into condemnation; but is passed from death unto life.
>
> Romans 6 v 23 : For the wages of sin is death; but the gift of God is eternal life through Jesus Christ our Lord.
>
> Romans 10 v 9 : If thou shalt confess with thy mouth the Lord Jesus, and shalt believe in thine heart that God raised him from the dead, thou shalt be saved.

God could not break his promises and it was wrong to doubt those promises. The reality of that truth went deep down inside the young boy and he never again doubted his salvation.

Charlie's years in Glasgow took him not only to assemblies of church folk but also showed him what life was like in the poorer areas of the city. He became a Sunday School teacher at the age of 17. His own Bible class mentor was Jack Ferguson, a man whom he described later in life as the single most influential person in his formative years. Much as Charlie enjoyed increasing his Bible knowledge—an enjoyment which would lead eventually to a Master's degree—he learnt from Jack Ferguson and others that 'head knowledge' of Scripture was of little value unless it made a difference in his life. Only then could he share the good news of Jesus with real conviction.

By now the war clouds were dark over Europe and before the end of that war Charlie's path would be firmly set in new directions. Before we pursue them, however, we can look back through his own recollections of life as a young boy growing up in St Helens.

Chapter 2

SNAPSHOTS FROM SCHOOLDAYS

Charlie was nearly four years old. It was 1926, the year of the General Strike, but far more distressing to his memory than any economic, industrial or political troubles of the time was an incident he recalled years later.

He was a new pupil at a small private kindergarten school in a double-fronted house across the road from where he lived. Wearing his new blue blazer with brass buttons, he set off as usual one bright September morning. No sooner had the big front door of their house closed behind him than, to his horror, he realised that he did not have with him the biscuit which he was allowed to consume at 10.30 a.m. precisely. Thinking that he might starve to death before lunchtime at noon, he turned to ring the door-bell, but finding that he could not reach it, he began to knock frantically on the heavy door with clenched fists, calling out in anguish, 'My biscuit! My biscuit! I've forgotten my biscuit!'

His wailing was all in vain. In his despair it did not occur to him to go round to the back of the house. With smarting knuckles and on the point of tears, young Charlie negotiated the garden gate and crossed the road, nearly getting himself knocked down by a group of men cycling to work.

The Reverend Bernard Woolley, a short, stout clergyman, who lodged at the school and always left on his pastoral rounds as the pupils arrived, tried to comfort the boy, but ecclesiastical consolation was not enough.

Miss Phyllis, a thin girl of eighteen or so, who supervised shoe-changing in the dimly lit corridor, listened sympathetically to the tragic tale and, as if by magic, instantly produced three-quarters of a digestive biscuit from the pocket of her pinafore. She blew off the fluff and held it out at arm's length with a triumphant grin. Charlie seized it gratefully, even though it was smaller than the customary Abernethy, and in his delight and excitement crammed it into his mouth.

His ecstasy was short-lived. The impressive figure of Miss Hall, the headmistress, loomed over him.

'I'm surprised at you, David Oxley,' she said sharply, 'eating your biscuit before the proper time.' (She always mixed him up with his brother and he sensed that this was probably not the best occasion on which to correct her.) 'You are a greedy boy, a very greedy boy.'

He began to explain... 'Don't speak with your mouth full,' she snapped.

'But Miss...'

Miss Phyllis mercifully snatched him away.

'Really!' exclaimed Miss Hall indignantly but to nobody in particular. 'I don't know what children are coming to nowadays, I really don't.'

Later, while arranging burnt-out match-sticks into the shape of a house, he puzzled over this remark and pondered on the injustice of it all. The conclusion that he reached was that he liked Miss Phyllis, that he did not like Miss Hall, and that in future he would try to remember his biscuit.

§

THE INFANTS DEPARTMENT of Rivington Road Elementary School, which Charlie attended from 1927 to 1929, was ruled over by Miss

Thompson, a short, square woman, who seemed to spend most of her school day slapping wrists.

The children of the school used to play 'bell horses' in pairs with arms linked behind their backs as they galloped around with knees up high. One afternoon, Charlie and his partner were feeling adventurous, so they pranced out of the school gates and on to the road. They had their wrists smartly smacked for 'making an exhibition' of themselves.

Empire Day approached—May 24th—a day of thanksgiving, pride and rejoicing. With mounting excitement, the pupils prepared to celebrate the great day by dressing up in the national costumes of the many countries of the British Empire and dancing round a maypole. Because Charlie's mother was of Scottish ancestry and there was a kilt available, plus plaid and full regalia, he was to represent Scotland.

After morning assembly prayers and Bible story, each child was given a large sheet of white paper on which to draw a Union Jack. Becoming bored with shading in vast expanses of red and blue triangles, Charlie drew a small piglet, knowing that it would soon be obliterated by red crayon. Unfortunately, he was rather lacking in creative skills, and Miss Thompson, perhaps suspicious of his increased concentration, looked over his shoulder and spied the offending animal. This effort at artistic originality she interpreted as an act of gross disrespect to king and country. The ensuing slapping of wrists was particularly severe, born as it was of deep patriotic fervour.

On the morning of the great day itself, there was much frustration as the children tried desperately to perfect the intertwining of the red, white and blue ribbons in an intricate pattern. It was quite beyond them.

A turbanned representative of India the brightest jewel in the British Crown, had his cocoa-dyed wrists soundly smacked for deliberately tripping up a little girl in Welsh costume, causing her tall conical black hat to roll crazily on the ground.

During a lull in rehearsals, Billy Higginbottom, dressed as a Red Indian chieftain, became inquisitive about what was under Charlie's kilt and tried to investigate. Instantly defending Scottish honour, Charlie grabbed the cardboard tomahawk from Billy's belt and with a mighty swing would surely have decapitated him had he not ducked. The feathers of his head-dress fluttered in all directions. Another fearful swipe of the tomahawk knocked the clay pipe of peace out of Billy's hand to shatter in a hundred pieces on the concrete flags. Billy's howls, which were very Red Indian, brought Miss Thompson bustling to the battle scene.

More wrist slapping. Miss Thompson made the boys shake hands and pick up the pieces of the clay pipe. The tears made streaks down Billy's painted face. With tomahawk smashed and feathers flattened, this miniature Indian brave looked a sorry sight.

The grand finale of the day was to form a big circle in the school hall, to hold up their Union Jacks and to sing, loudly and proudly, *Rule Britannia, Land of Hope and Glory* and *God save the King*, with Miss Farrington banging out the familiar chords on the school piano. Empire Day ended with three cheers, followed by strict instructions to take home all their belongings.

'And woe betide anyone who leaves anything behind,' warned Miss Thompson. The children did not understand the 'woe betide' bit, but they guessed that it meant big trouble if they forgot anything.

The Empire Day celebrations had been intended to foster pride in the achievement of bringing civilised behaviour to millions around the world. In the process the teachers had made noble efforts to inculcate similarly civilised behaviour in the Infants Department of Rivington Road Elementary School.

§

ON CHARLIE'S SEVENTH BIRTHDAY a large, well-wrapped parcel arrived by post from Glasgow. Auntie Jeannie, his mother's sister, had sent him one of those heavy volumes called *Bumper Annual*; it had stiff cardboard covers, stories, pictures, poems and puzzles, and was at least three inches thick.

The front cover presented the problem. It showed a brightly coloured picture of an incredibly clean, rosy-cheeked boy and girl, both about five years old, playing with a kitten in a garden. The title, written in large, flowing letters, was *Our Darlings*.

Maiden aunts who see their nephews and nieces only once or twice a year tend to underestimate their rate of development through childhood to adolescence. To send *Our Darlings* to a seven-year-old boy was an unfortunate example of this fond misapprehension. The contents of the book offered hours of enjoyable reading; it was the title page which caused the consternation.

'You must take your present to school to show your teacher,' said Charlie's mother brightly. All his excuses—'It's too heavy to carry to school', or 'The teacher won't have time to read it', or 'She'll think it's soppy'—were brushed aside with a 'Nonsense, dear. She'll be delighted.'

And so it was that Charlie set off with a heavy book and a heavier heart on the one-mile walk to school. His teacher, Miss Jones, was a young lady engaged to be married to Mr Hatton, who taught Standard 5. (The same young lady had given Charlie a kiss on one occasion when he got all his spellings right.) Miss Jones admired his present and told him he was a very fortunate boy.

The route to and from Rivington Road School led past St Teresa's Roman Catholic School and there was often some name-calling and occasionally a fight. Almost inevitably, as Charlie approached St Teresa's on his homeward walk at four o'clock, he noticed with some alarm a group of boys larking about in the road. Hoping to pass by unnoticed, he proceeded cautiously but was quickly spotted and surrounded. The largest of the group, a well-known bully with the nickname 'Quackie', seized the book and with exaggerated derision read out the title—'*Our Darlings*'.

'Our Darlings!' he repeated in a loud and mocking voice. 'Our Darlings!!' The others fell about laughing raucously and, as if on cue, began circling round Charlie in an impromptu dance, chanting 'Our darlings! Our darlings!' It started like ring-a-ring-a-roses in clogs but quickly became more menacing, a grotesque tribal war dance.

In response to Charlie's repeated demand of 'Give it back to me,' Quackie held out the book tauntingly, saying, "Ere you are, darlin'; come and gerrit.'

Whether the red of embarrassment was more in evidence than the white of anger we shall never know, but in his rage Charlie grabbed the great tome from Quackie's grasp. Holding it high above his head with both hands, he brought it crashing down on Quackie's head with a tremendous thump. Quackie's eyes crossed, his knees buckled and he sank to the ground. His pals gasped in disbelief, but Charlie was off, running for home and safety as fast as his little legs would carry him, without a backward glance.

§

SATURDAY 16TH NOVEMBER 1929 was a date Charlie never forgot. Sombre grey clouds hung over the smoke-wreathed industrial town of St Helens, a town famous for the manufacture not only of glass but also of Beecham's pills, sold in round wooden boxes for sixpence, but according to the label 'worth a guinea a box'.

Helen, aged six and a half, with Charlie, who was fourteen months older, had been taken by their parents in their black box-like Jowett saloon car to the department store which they owned and ran in the centre of the town. The children were to be fitted with new shoes and Helen, rosy-cheeked and with her fair hair in long pigtails, relished every moment of this excursion.

At about mid-day she and Charlie were despatched on the fifteen-minute tram ride home for lunch, boarding at Sefton Arms and asking for 'two halves to the Bird I'th' Hand.' (Most of the stops were at public houses.) The tram jolted, rattled and swayed round into Bridge Street, past familiar little shops in Liverpool Road—now no more—up the steep incline of Croppers Hill and along Prescot Road.

At the Bird I'th' Hand, Charlie and Helen alighted and started to cross the main road, but the departing tram obscured their view of an oncoming lorry. They had reached the middle of the road before seeing the lorry heading straight for them. They both ran and Charlie reached safety, but Helen, running away from the vehicle but still in its path, was knocked down. Someone screamed. Charlie looked round horrified to see Helen spinning beneath the lorry, its tyres screeching on the shiny stone sets.

He ran to where Helen lay unconscious. Her blue eyes were wide open, looking at him sightlessly as if to say, 'Why did you let me get run over?'

Three or four people appeared as from nowhere. The dreaded word 'hospital' was spoken urgently. Charlie turned and ran the hundred and twenty yards home to tell the awful news as quickly as he could. Breathlessly he gasped out the story to Winnie, the maid.

'Oh Lor'!' she wailed. 'Oh Lor'!' Tearing off her apron, she ran out of the house towards the scene of the accident, shouting 'Stay there!' over her shoulder. He stayed.

Soon Winnie returned, red-faced and panting. 'Not a sign,' she gasped as she ran into the morning room to telephone Charlie's mother at the shop. Holding the ear-piece in a trembling hand, she frantically turned the little black handle of the then fashionable instrument.

When the soup-plates brimming with home-made Scotch broth appeared on the kitchen table for Charlie and his older brother, it was the first and probably the only time in his young life that he could not eat his dinner.

It was mid-afternoon and beginning to grow dark when the car trundled into the yard and Mr and Mrs Oxley came in with the news that the lorry driver's mate had picked Helen up in his arms and they had driven her in the lorry—it belonged to Gallie's, the wine merchants in Market Street—straight to the Providence Hospital, which was run by Roman Catholic nursing sisters.

They had just caught a glimpse of Helen being wheeled into the operating theatre. 'The puir wee thing was as white as a sheet,' was all Charlie's mother could say. She kept repeating 'The puir wee thing' to give some consolation to whoever heard her. Charlie sat, quiet and anxious, fully expecting at least a good telling-off for letting his sister get run over, but nobody said anything to suggest that he was to blame.

He was in his pyjamas ready for bed when he was summoned to the drawing-room. A large policeman with a big moustache sat in an armchair, his helmet between his boots on the tiger skin rug. Seeing the boy's evident alarm, he said reassuringly, 'It's all right, sonny. Just a few questions.' Holding a tiny stub of pencil in his huge hand, he wrote down Charlie's answers.

At last he said, 'There y'are then,' and, handing his pencil and notebook to the bemused boy, said, 'Sign it, if you please, sonny.' Charlie looked at the pencil, frowned at the notebook and wondered what he had to do. 'Just write your name there,' explained the policeman, much to the lad's relief.

On Sunday mornings the family always went to 'the meeting', but the following Sunday they set off early so as to call at the hospital, which was just behind the Central Hall where the 'meetings' were held. Charlie and his brother David waited in the echoing corridor as father and mother were led into the children's ward by a sister dressed more like a nun than a nurse. A large statue of Jesus with bleeding wounds did nothing to soothe the boys' anxieties.

They were eventually called to walk carefully across the highly polished wood-block floor to a white-railed cot in which Helen lay with her head heavily bandaged but smiling faintly. Charlie was aware of many pairs of eyes watching him and he wondered whether they were silently accusing him of letting his sister get run over. One of the lorry's wheels had run over her upper arm and shoulder. She had a splintered fracture of the right upper arm and collar bone and her right ear had been partly torn off. Mr Oxley hung a daily tear-off text calendar over Helen's cot and remarked on the appropriateness of the day's verse—'The Lord bless thee and keep thee.'

On the Sunday afternoon, after Sunday School, father went to thank the driver and his mate for their prompt action, which the surgeon said had saved her life. He came home saying that the driver was a man in his fifties and his nerves had been shattered by the accident. For the ten weeks that Helen lay in hospital, the driver called every Saturday afternoon just before visiting time with a small paper bag of dolly mixtures or jelly babies.

Soon after Helen came home from the hospital, pale and thin and 'in need of fattening up', the family heard that the lorry driver had collapsed and died quite suddenly. Mr and Mrs Oxley went to the funeral and on their return told the family that the driver's widow had said, 'It was the accident, you know. He never got over it.'

§

A STRICT BRETHREN UPBRINGING entailed frequent attendance at gospel meetings, ministry meetings, Bible readings, and conferences on Saturdays and bank holidays. It also entailed, on occasions, some difficulties with those from different backgrounds. The schools Charlie attended were staffed by teachers who were sympathetic to the Christian faith in its broadest sense, if not to biblical fundamentalism in its narrower sense.

One day, in the Standard 3 class of nine-year-olds, Mr Wolfe started a lesson on 'proverbs' by asking the class of 40 boys for examples. Charlie's hand shot up.

'Well, Oxley, what's your proverb?' asked Mr Wolfe, a tall, well-built man with a large brown moustache.

'Please, sir, "My son, if sinners entice thee, consent not to them".'

'That's not a proverb,' drawled the teacher scornfully.

'Please, sir, yes it is. It's in the Book of Proverbs, chapter one, verse ten. I learned it for Sunday School, sir.'

Charlie was not over-fond of Mr Wolfe. He was constantly nagging at him to pull up his socks or get his hair out of his eyes. The boy's secret delight at scoring one over him must have shown itself.

'For your information, Oxley, we are dealing with English proverbs, not Bible proverbs,' replied Mr Wolfe with heavy sarcasm.

Other boys trotted out commonplace half-truths about 'too many cooks,' 'making hay' and 'all that glitters', but Charlie felt that his was much superior. He made a conscious decision at that moment to dislike English proverbs—an antipathy he was inclined to extend to people who quoted them.

Forty years later, when intellectuals on a radio programme referred to the Bible text, 'To the pure all things are pure,' as a 'motto', a 'maxim', a 'cliché' and a 'proverb', showing total misunderstanding of its content and meaning, his indignation drove him to write a strongly worded letter of complaint to the BBC. As was the case with so many such complaints, the response was a polite brush-off.

Mr Kermode, nicknamed 'Daddy', was the head of the Cowley Junior School at Windlehurst. He was an excellent teacher who endeared himself to Charlie by instantly handing him his large white handkerchief one day when he had a sudden nose bleed.

He gave the class a lesson on Jacob and Esau in which the deceitfulness of Jacob gaining an unfair advantage over his brother to obtain the birthright and blessing was stressed as a dire warning to all who practise lies and deceit. At the end of the lesson he asked the class of about twenty-four boys which of the two brothers was the more honourable. Everyone except Charlie put his hand up in favour of Esau.

'Well, Oxley,' asked Mr Kermode with genuine interest, 'what's your problem?'

'Please, sir, it says in the Bible that God said, "Jacob have I loved, Esau have I hated".'

Accepting his claim, Mr Kermode asked, 'And why do you think God preferred Jacob?'

'I dunno, sir. God moves in a mysterious way, sir.'

'He sure does, Oxley; he sure does.'

Chapter 3

TEACHING, MARRIAGE AND TOWER COLLEGE

Towards the end of the war Charlie found himself training as a purser in the Merchant Navy. His accident had put an end to his Fire Service days, but during his recuperation he had studied Hebrew and developed his love of books. He particularly enjoyed reading of the great Christian missionaries such as Hudson Taylor, William Carey and C T Studd. He himself had a heart to see the gospel proclaimed across the nations, but his view of the world was so far limited to the town of St Helens and the city of Glasgow.

There was therefore definitely something of 'join-the-navy-and-see-the-world' that prompted Charlie to enlist with the Anchor Line, who sent him on

It was during his time as a purser in the Merchant Navy that Charles left to embark on his teaching career at Victoria College in Alexandria, Egypt.

the m.v. *Cilicia* and the s.s. *Tarantia* to various West African ports, but mostly on the India run, through the Mediterranean and the Suez Canal. The pace of dock work in some of these ports was extremely slow, so while waiting for cargo to be unloaded and loaded, Charlie seized the opportunity to look around these cities and gain a little insight into the way of life of local people. He also maintained a disciplined programme of study, for he had set his mind to gaining a degree and becoming a schoolmaster.

Meanwhile, his family's move to Glasgow had not diminished the long friendship between the Oxleys and the Choletons, even though they now lived far apart. Helen Oxley was still a close friend of Nora Cholerton and when visits were arranged between their respective homes in Glasgow and St Helens, other members of both families were included. Perhaps a certain amount of absence had made one heart grow fonder, for it dawned on Charlie during one leave just how attractive young Muriel Cholerton was. He began to see more of her during his times on leave, even though their friendship evoked a mixed reaction from other members of their families.

Muriel had grown up to be a photographer in the family business, although during the war she served as a nurse. When the war ended she returned to her photography and when she went off to fulfil a wedding assignment, if Charlie was home on leave, he would accompany her. He particularly admired her efficiency in dealing with blushing brides and disorganised family groups and it required no huge leap of imagination to see himself walking down the aisle one day with this delightful young lady. In addition to her natural charms, he saw that they shared strong Christian faith, self-discipline and a capacity for hard work. Both of them had grown up in a family which had built up successful businesses from small beginnings.

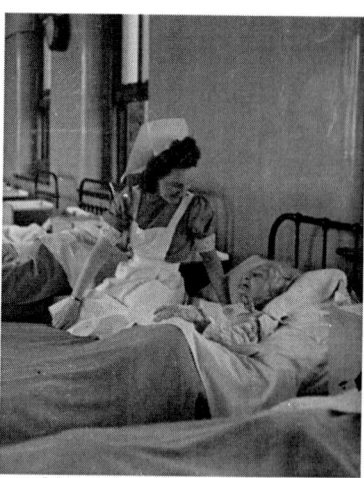

Muriel in her war-time service of nursing, from which she returned to the family photography business.

All these thoughts made each return to Charlie's ship an agony, with the prospect of another lengthy voyage only adding to the pain of parting. Those who knew Charles Oxley only in later life as a tireless crusader and educationalist might be surprised to learn of this romantic side to his character, but it clearly survived the stringencies of a Brethren upbringing.

Almost daily he wrote home to 'my dear Muriel' about how much he was missing her and looking forward to seeing her again. Postal deliveries to Indian ports in 1946 were less than regular, so it would sometimes be over a week that he would have to agonise without receiving a letter from her; then, like London buses, two or three would arrive together.

Charlie's mother and brother David strongly disapproved of his relationship with Muriel; even the friendship between sister Helen and Muriel's sister Nora cooled considerably because of some nasty remarks made about Muriel. Although Charlie was geographically far removed from it all, he felt the pain of it in Muriel's letters and it made him all the more angry that she was suffering unfair criticism when he was not there to try and put things right. He expressed strong feelings in his letters, though, especially when his mother and brother suggested that the relationship would damage his spiritual welfare. 'I'm sick and tired of their simpering vindictiveness' was how he put it in a letter to Muriel. 'They don't favour it for selfish reasons and are resorting to lies, false accusations and anything else to cause a break.'

Further family disapproval centred on Charlie's plans for the future, quite apart from the fact that Muriel now featured very much in those plans. He felt sure he could find a teaching post in India or Egypt, which would enable him to go on studying for his degree. By acquiring teaching experience abroad he would be able to by-pass the longer process of teacher training in Britain, followed by a probationary year. To the insular, conservative thinking of his mother this seemed utter madness, but Charlie was not to be deterred.

He made enquiries about teaching jobs in India and wrote to British embassies in Port Said and Cairo. He wrote to his mother 'to put her in her place', telling her that he and Muriel were 'waiting on the Lord to open up the way.' Almost immediately he received a cable: 'Please cable earliest possible commence duty Port Said and salary required. Mention next port of call and date. British School.' He asked around among his acquaintances who had lived in Egypt as to the cost of living and therefore the kind of salary he could justifiably expect to be paid. Much would depend also on the kind of accommodation available; as he wrote to Muriel: 'If God provides a home in Port Said and a salary sufficient to cover everything, then I think that's a strong indication that He has opened up the way for us.'

Nevertheless, it seems that Port Said was not his preferred target. 'I've made up my mind to write to the British Embassy in Egypt asking them to put me in touch with the British schools in Alexandria and Cairo.'

During tedious voyages he had plenty of time to dream of his future in teaching and to defend some of his beliefs against those of his non-Christian shipmates. He wrote in September 1946 from the m.v. *Tarantia* in Bombay: 'We had a great discussion tonight on the Creation or the Theory of Evolution. It is a terrible shame that it is allowed to be taught in schools. Much good and much harm can be done by schoolteachers—so here's hoping I manage to do some good. I'm looking forward to getting settled down in the teaching profession.'

A few days later he wrote: 'I've no fears for the future. I feel sure I'll get fixed up somewhere before long. Then I'll get cracking for the degree, which with the teaching experience will qualify me for a good post at home. I think it would be rather nice to teach in Cowley.' That was the grammar school he attended in St Helens.

In early October 1946 he was invited to tea with the Headmaster of Karachi Grammar School who offered him a job teaching English and History. He applied also to a large Commercial College and was offered a teaching job there; he would perhaps be able to supplement his salary with some evening classes and private tuition. Yet still he did not feel he had found the right opening.

More than once, when his ship was ready to return to the U K, plans were changed and they had to take another cargo to another foreign port. The frustration stood out clearly in his letters home: 'I like sailing and I like seeing different places and speaking to different people but I do not like chasing all around the globe when we are supposed to be going home!'

He was quite prepared, though, to try his hand at new experiences. 'In the Arabian Sea I asked the Captain if I could help with the navigating and he agreed... so I've been doing my stuff with sextants, compasses, charts, chronometers and things.'

Three days after sending this letter, on October 16th, he received the telegram which would settle him in his first teaching post and lead to a lifetime of educational enterprise. He in turn sent a telegram to Muriel to give her the glad tidings: 'COMPELLED TO LEAVE SHIP TO SECURE EXCELLENT APPOINTMENT MASTER VICTORIA COLLEGE ALEXANDRIA.'

Within a fortnight he was home on leave with an engagement ring in his pocket and a host of plans in his mind. Ten days later he and Muriel were married.

A long engagement was hardly necessary as they had known each other from earliest childhood and their families had been so close over the years. The opposition from some of their relatives probably made young Charlie even more determined to go through with a relationship which both heart and head told him was right. Also, he could see little point in being away in Alexandria and pining for Muriel back home. As it happened, that was how their married life began, because, although he was able to leave the Merchant Navy immediately to accept the post at Victoria College, Muriel's visa to go and join him did not materialise for several months.

Victoria College in Alexandria was founded in 1902, a year after the death of the Queen from whom it took its name. It claimed to be unique for being the first school in the western world to educate kings and princes. Previously, heirs to the throne, from the era of the Pharaohs onwards, had been assumed to have been born with all the attributes of education and these simply needed to be refined by governesses and tutors within the royal palace. In 1902, however, when Britannia ruled the waves and Britain ruled the Empire, Egypt basked in the sunshine of occupation. The clerks of the future had to be trained, in the British Boys' School, to serve the state; and a Victoria College had to be founded to educate the future rulers of state. In the words of an early prospectus: 'Victoria College was founded with the object of affording residents in Egypt the opportunity of giving their sons an education similar to that of the English Public Schools.'

Charles Oxley, sometime store assistant, fireman and purser, knew how fortunate he was, as an untrained Englishman, to secure a teaching post at such a prestigious seat of learning. By the time he joined the staff, the reputation of the College had spread far and wide, so that royalty and nobility from many countries sent their sons to be educated there. A total of seventy-six nationalities were represented while Charles was there.

His first letter to Muriel, dated 30th November, showed that her husband was not in the least overawed by such exalted company: 'The school is full of all sorts of queer folk. We have Jews, Arabs, Egyptians, Syrians, Poles, Sudanese, Yugoslavs, Greeks and English. Amongst the nobility in my dormitory are the ex-King of Bulgaria, the Sultan of Madagascar and the son of the Egyptian Prime Minister.'

Noble blood was no guarantee of high intellect. 'The class I've just taken has in it the son of the Sudanese Prime Minister. He's very thick.'

The varied backgrounds of his pupils guaranteed Charles some delightful howlers. The Upper 4th had been talking too much in one lesson, so he had them write out twenty-five times each: 'A man of understanding holdeth his peace.' One of the boys, understandably unfamiliar with the quaintness of 17th century English, reproduced this as: 'A man of understanding hold death his peas.'

Many of the staff had taught in British public schools or had ambitions to do so. Although they accepted the Lancastrian/Glaswegian well enough, he found them—and especially their accents—'too much on the lah-de-dah side. The jolly old Oxford, by gad, sir. What?'

Charles established a disciplined pattern to his life, rising early to put in several hours of study each day in addition to his teaching duties. He saw at close quarters the clash of Christianity with Islam and grasped the opportunity to teach the Christian faith to a group of boys who came along week by week to his Bible class. As he wrote to an old friend in Glasgow, 'There is great opportunity for much work here—it is the centre of Mohammedanism, which I regard as Satan's counter-attack to the way of salvation. It is a counterfeit in every respect.'

He visited El Alamein less than four years after the battle which made that name synonymous with the war in North Africa. He gazed in silence along the neat lines of graves—7,781 of the Allies and a similar number of Italian or German troops. So many dead in just four days.

In January 1947 he received a letter from his mother purporting to prove from the Scriptures that it was God's will for him to stay in Britain and not go to Egypt. She referred to Moses, Jethro, Daniel, Ezra, Nehemiah, Jeremiah, John and Theophilus. Charles remained unimpressed and unconvinced by this wrenching of Scripture to make it say what she wanted it to say. He wrote to Muriel that in his reply he had asked his mother whether 'she could prove that her action was right by the Scripture, namely her treatment of you.'

On Muriel's part, the long wait for a visa did make her question whether they had done the right thing. As for Charles, in his perplexity he asked God to show him a reason for this delay; the answer he received was that he was in danger of putting his love for Muriel before his love for God. He needed to focus clearly on putting God first in his life. As he did that, he made the delightful discovery that to obey the greatest commandment, to love God with all his heart, soul, mind and strength, did not diminish his love for Muriel one iota.

Eventually the visa arrived and Muriel joined Charles in Alexandria on May 1st, five and a half months after their wedding. She stayed for one term, sharing her husband's busy life and realising that marriage to this man would leave little time for leisurely diversions. The word 'workaholic' was yet to be invented, but whoever coined it must surely have had Charles Oxley in mind. He was still studying for several hours a day in addition to his teaching, marking, preparing and housemastering, and still running a Scripture Union class for the boys.

Sport occupied as important a place in the life of Victoria College as it did in any English public school. Charles had never given much time to sport, but he certainly enjoyed athletics, rugby and cricket. In his time at Cowley Grammar School in St Helens, a hotbed of rugby talent in both Union and League modes, his long legs and large hands had enabled him to become a very useful wing three-quarter. On the running track he proved to be a speedy sprinter.

It was his cricketing prowess, however, which Muriel was to witness in the annual Staff v Boys match. Charles was eagerly looking forward to showing his bride what he could do with a bat; she for her part could not wait to applaud his innings. The outcome—bowled first ball—kept the young man humble and the young lady quietly amused!

In July they both returned to England, staying with Muriel's parents in St Helens. What began as a casual conversation in that home was to have far-reaching consequences. Muriel's niece, Janet, had just turned four years of age. She was the daughter of Muriel's eldest sister, Pauline, and her husband William Butler.

'Which school will Janet be going to?' asked Mrs Cholerton.

'We're not really sure yet,' said Pauline. 'We've thought about one or two of the local primary schools but none of them really take our fancy.'

'Well, Charlie,' said Muriel, 'why don't you start your own private school?'

It may have been said half-jokingly at first, but soon the idea caught on in his mind. He prayed about it and talked it over with Muriel. There were very few private schools in the St Helens area, so there could well be families willing to pay modest fees to have their children educated privately, even in such industrialised parts with strong support for the Labour party. He had formulated his own educational philosophy and principles, and the Butler Education Act of 1944 had pointed the way forward for schools in the post-war years. Charles' idealism was supported by his own and Muriel's solid business background and they soon began to plan seriously the setting up of a private school.

The first consideration was to find a suitable property. Muriel's father mentioned a mansion in Mill Lane, called The Towers. It had served as a hospital in the Second World War and was owned by a Mr Forester, who lived in half the building and was willing to sell the other half. Charles took Muriel to have a look, knowing that they had little time before Charles would have to return to Alexandria to work the requisite term's notice.

Their tour of the property showed that the whole house could well be converted into a school, but as yet they could only afford half of it, which was all that Mr Forester was willing to sell. He used the other half of the building both to live in and as a mini-factory for producing a popular drink called 'Number Ten Cocktail'. He had crates of the stuff piled high in the house. 'If I sell all this lot,' he told them, 'I'll give you the other half of the house for nothing.'

The unoccupied half of the house was pretty dilapidated; when Charles and Muriel first looked inside the front door, the floor had fallen through to the cellar and trees were growing in at the upstairs windows. The potential private school proprietors were certainly starting at the bottom as they began to build their life's work together. Undeterred, they made an offer of £1,600, but it was only as Charles was driving away from The Towers that Mr Forester ran after the car to agree the sale.

Charles returned to Victoria College leaving Muriel to cope with all the repairs and renovations, the fabric and the furnishing of what was to become Tower College. This was some workload for a 22-year-old, married less than a year, while her husband was away in Egypt, but her resilience and determination came through strongly. Like Charles, she had a visionary zeal for sound Christian education which continually motivated her through all the pressures of that period. Without that zeal, the whole project would have failed.

When Charles told some of his colleagues at Victoria College about his plans, several of them expressed an interest in joining him in the venture. He unexpectedly had plenty of time to work on his ideas for the new school, because a serious cholera outbreak in Alexandria affected attendance at the College. He busily worked on class sizes, termly fees, daily timetables. He considered that eight guineas per term would be the right fee for the under-7s, rising to 13 guineas for the 11-to-14-year-olds.

Muriel's first letter since his return to Egypt reached him on October 5th 1947. Contracts for the sale of The Towers had still not been signed, but happily the local council had approved their request to change the use of the premises to a school. He in Egypt and she in England were constantly on the lookout for desks, chairs, books and other essentials. Since Tower College would be their home as well as their school, Charles searched the shops and stalls of Alexandria for domestic furniture as well—dining chairs, suites, bookcases. He was buying curtains and carpets while she was attending to floorboards, electrics and the plastering of walls.

As if she did not already have enough on her mind, Muriel then received confirmation that she was expecting a baby. Charles had no doubts—it would be a girl; in several letters home in the later months of 1947 he referred to 'Judith'. Despite his certainty, they produced three sons before their only daughter appeared, and they gave her the name of Rachel!

The cholera outbreak worsened; in just one day in October there were 145 deaths in Alexandria.

A married couple called Callow were very keen to work for Charles in the projected new school, the husband teaching Geography, Woodwork and P.E., his wife teaching French and working in the office. With the help of a trusted lady called Mrs Henstock, Charles felt sure he would have all the help he needed initially, as he intended to take the other subjects himself.

He found it very frustrating to be away from Muriel just when there was so much to do to make The Towers ready. 'This separation really is the last. There's to be DEFINITELY NO MORE!!!' he wrote. He even thought about them having a holiday together, acknowledging that their summer holiday 'wasn't a success because I got fed-up so easily. I wonder if we'll ever get a real holiday together. We'll need to. Where would you like to go?' They had never had a proper honeymoon, of course, but as the busy tempo of their married life became established, holidays came well down the list of priorities. In his later years, with three schools and large numbers of staff, he felt on the one hand that teachers' holidays were too long, but on the other hand he grasped the opportunities that those weeks of non-term-time gave him to pursue his other commitments with fewer interruptions.

Charles was still proving his worth at Victoria College, even though he was looking forward so much to returning to England at Christmas. During his final term in Alexandria he was given charge of the reception dormitory. This gave him practice in paternal duties, as he was the houseparent for all new arrivals, none of whom spoke a word of English. He therefore had to give them all their instructions in Arabic, which he evidently managed to do with minimal fuss and great success. These new boys were kept apart from the other pupils for a time while they learnt the College routines and rules, so Charles had to check their clothing, teach them, feed them and exercise them.

The Headmaster was loth to lose such a fine member of staff. As the end of term approached, he called Charles in to see him.

'Are you quite sure you're doing the right thing in starting up your own school?' he asked. 'You're still very young, you know, and you could make an excellent career for yourself.'

'Yes, I'm quite sure,' said Charles. 'My wife and I have bought a property and preparations are well under way.'

'I'll be honest with you, Oxley. I don't want to lose you; you've done very well in your time here.'

'Thank you, sir.'

'If you'll stay I'll give you a promotion and a salary increase.'

'That's very kind of you, sir, but my mind is made up and the plans are too far advanced.'

'Mmm. Oh well, good luck to you, Oxley.'

The jobs back home were piling up and Charles was itching to get busy. He borrowed an expression of Muriel's father—'I'll swipe 'em'—which typified his eagerness to be involved in the Tower preparations. Part of his frustration had been the length of time it took for a letter from Muriel to reach him and let him know what was happening with builders, electricians, plasterers and the like, and then the time it took for his reply to reach her so that she could do what he suggested.

There were moments too when their finances seemed to be strained to the limit. As the bills mounted up, Charles wrote to Muriel that they must 'keep repairs etc. to the bare minimum.' In the back of their minds they knew that they could, as Muriel had pointed out to him, 'always sell the whole place if we get into a jam.'

Even the cost of transporting furniture from Alexandria to Liverpool turned out to be much more than expected. Charles had been quoted a figure of £36 by one company, but in the end it cost him £150 to have all his belongings packed into a crate and shipped back to England. He himself flew from Cairo at 10.30 p.m. on December 23rd, landing in London at 2.30 p.m. on Christmas Eve.

The New Year—1948—saw two significant births for Charles and Muriel: their first child—Marcus Alexander—arrived and their first school—Tower College—opened for its first pupils in September.

Mr Forester had changed his business interests from cocktails to potato crisps in the other half of The Towers, partly because of a few problems with the health department of the local authority. He became successful enough to move his operations into a proper factory and so gave the Oxleys the option of buying his half of The Towers for £2000. All their capital had gone into buying and renovating their original half, plus the expense of fitting out the rooms to be used for the school. However, Muriel's sister Nora and her husband Jimmy generously sold the deeds of their house and lent the money to Charles and Muriel.

Marcus, the eldest of four children, pictured during the first term of the newly-established Tower College, with proud parents/proprietors Charles, 26, and Muriel, 23.

The Towers, Rainhill, Merseyside: home base and first school – Tower College – set up by Charles and Muriel in 1948.

Few people achieve anything significant in life without first dreaming about it; even fewer see the fulfilment of their dreams by the age of 26. Charles Oxley had for years seen himself becoming a schoolmaster, though only in the recent past had he visualised owning and running his own school. As yet he had neither degree nor teaching qualification, and his teaching experience was limited to a year at Victoria College, Alexandria. How could he possibly expect parents to entrust their children to his care for their education in those precious formative years? What he did have were enthusiasm, abundant energy and very clear ideas as to what comprised a sound Christian education.

Some of his earlier ideas had been refined or jettisoned. He had toyed with the idea of making Tower College into a preparatory school with the aim of feeding pupils into public schools at 13 years of age. He had written from Egypt to Muriel that such an aim 'adds "class" to the place ... I'm sure this will be a big advantage and will make for having a really posh type of child.' In the event, Tower College quickly established a reputation for high academic standards and strict discipline, yet without losing its 'family' feeling, which still remains today. This came about not just because school rooms and Oxley family rooms shared the same building, but also because Charles and Muriel gave themselves as wholeheartedly to the upbringing of other people's children as they did to their own. Each of their four children followed cousin Janet into Tower's classrooms without expecting or receiving any special favours.

By the time Marcus was old enough to start school he already had a brother, Michael David, born in July 1950. There was then a gap of almost four years before the third son arrived—Daniel Charles, born in April 1954. And Marcus was two weeks short of his ninth birthday when Rachel Jane was born in March 1957.

Charles took his share of domestic chores. He had learnt how to darn socks during his Merchant Navy days and was not averse to cooking or washing up. He brought up the early morning cup of tea to the family and together they had morning prayers, the four children listening from their earliest years to the readings from Scripture Union's *Daily Bread* and sharing in the family prayer time.

Meal-times invariably meant quizzes and questions for the children: spelling, word games, Bible questions. Later on, it was the children who fired the questions at their father, reading out Bible verses in the hope that he would be unable to locate them correctly. He was rarely wrong, however, even with obscure verses from Leviticus or Ecclesiastes.

He played his full part also in the evening bath-time ritual: Muriel would wash and he would dry! Marcus, as the eldest child, had the responsibility of bringing everyone their cup of cocoa, for which he received sixpence a week. Bedtime was at 7p.m., the time when

Muriel and Charles in 1962 with Marcus (back), Michael (right), Danny (left) and Rachel.

prospective parents would arrive for their appointments with the Headmaster of Tower College. Any delaying tactics by the four children inevitably led to a red-faced encounter in dressing-gown and slippers with cooing adults.

Holidays were spent visiting favourite family haunts or going to see places of interest: Charles delighted in pointing out particular buildings for the children's benefit and explaining why they were there. If it was London, he would simply stop the car amidst the frenetic rush of tooting traffic to show them the sights. If it was in Scotland, he would show them where their grandparents had lived or he would point to buildings he had helped to save in his fireman days.

Wherever it was, in Wales or Cornwall, in a caravan or on the beach, Charles still wore his suit and tie. (Evidently Danny, the third son, carries on this family tradition: when he and Rachel flew on holiday into Orlando in 1988, with temperatures soaring, he was the only passenger on the plane wearing a tie, much to the amusement of the girl at passport control.)

Tower College flourished. Additional classrooms were built to cater for up to 400 children aged from 3 to 16. The hard-headed folk of the area, from St Helens, Warrington and the eastern fringes of Liverpool, recognised the value of investing in their children's future by paying for private school education. Thrift, hard work, self-sacrifice and the elimination of waste have always been central virtues in the Oxley scheme of things, not only for themselves but also for any teachers or parents who committed themselves to the life of Tower College. The school has grown again in the late 1990s, both numerically and in extra buildings. The success of the enterprise has not been consumer-led, but the school has set standards of excellence which parents prize enough to want to make them available to their children.

Chapter 4

SCHOOL PHILOSOPHY AND SCARISBRICK HALL

When a new Education Act was passed in the summer of 1944, it charted the territory not only for state schools but also for educational pioneers such as Charles Oxley. There was much talk, as the end of the Second World War approached, of 'facing the task of national reconstruction', and R A Butler's Education Act was seen as integral to this process. Meanwhile, the Beveridge Report outlining the ground-breaking Welfare State had already been published and the nation sensed a mood of relief, growing optimism and a determination to rebuild after the horrors of war.

National education, understandably neglected during the war years in favour of national survival, now came high on the political agenda; and it was a *national*, cross-party effort, with human values paramount and greater attention given to children with average and below average ability. It was laid down as a 'general principle to be observed by the Minister and the local education authorities... that, so far as is compatible with the provision of efficient instruction and training and the avoidance of unreasonable public expenditure, pupils are to be educated in accordance with the wishes of their parents.' (Education Act 1944, Part IV, Section 76)

Many of us have had personal experience of perhaps just two schools, so when we try to picture our ideal school, we are undoubtedly influenced by what we remember as being the good and the bad in the schools we attended. Charles Oxley could have started from absolute scratch in setting up his own school, but he too recalled his own schooldays and fully intended to implement some of the practices and many of the principles he remembered. In a magazine article, *Whatever Happened to Education?*, he painted a vivid picture of his own schooldays:—

> A shrill blast on a whistle brought us smartly to attention in the playground of the elementary school I attended in the late 1920s. We marched into the large bare classrooms and stood in our places until told to sit by teachers with whom no liberties were taken. Hooked over the blackboard was the item of standard teaching equipment which concentrated attention, silenced chatter and punished forgetfulness, unpunctuality and indiscipline of all kinds.
>
> The day began with a hymn, Bible reading and prayers—kneeling on the woodblock floor. First lesson was always Scripture. Bible stories were told and re-told by believing teachers and their moral lessons propounded with authority. The Ten Commandments were drummed into us and we memorised several Psalms, many texts and the Beatitudes.
>
> The same sureness of purpose and natural assumption of authority was evident in the grammar school I attended in the 1930s. The teachers' authority was unquestioned by either pupils or parents.
>
> Schools were expected to teach children as much as they could learn and make them behave properly. This, with some physical training and compulsory team games for character building was the limit of society's expectation. Parents were assumed to be responsible for their children's physical, cultural and moral wellbeing and most of them accepted this as their role.

Charles' educational philosophy had three underlying aims: each child should be encouraged to achieve the highest academic standards of which he or she was capable; each child should be encouraged to achieve self-discipline and good behaviour; each child should be taught the Christian faith by means of Bible-based assemblies and Scripture lessons. If that seems idealistic to a later generation, he was realistic enough to recognise that as many as 90% of the parents who sent their children to his schools were very keen on the first two aims and accepted 'the religious bit' as an unavoidable part of the package. Only a small proportion actively sought an evangelical Christian education for their children, although many more would happily subscribe to a sub-Christian 'folk faith'. This might involve a visit to one's parish church two or three times a year, a doffing of hats towards the established church for certain rites of passage, and a belief that the Sermon on the Mount was 'a good thing' for their children to be aware of, even if their parents did not live by it.

What seemed to Charles to be a failing in the 1944 Education Act was the divisiveness of the 11+ examination. He felt that the Intelligence Test prevented many children from having the benefits of a grammar school education who might well have made a success of it. He felt that if children had been properly taught the basics of reading, writing and number work in their primary schools, a sizeable majority could and should have a grammar school type of education. What increasingly dismayed him in the 1970s and 1980s was the growing numbers of candidates for admission to his schools who clearly had the ability to cope with an academically rigorous education but had not been effectively taught the basics of Mathematics and English.

A straightforward test in these two subjects enabled any child from the age of 7 to gain admission to his schools. When he first began enrolling pupils for his third school—Hamilton College—in 1983, he was horrified at the general ineptitude of 11-year-olds who did not know, for example, what 'plural' meant. One boy, when asked to give the plural of 'potato' and told what 'plural' meant, gave as his answer 'chips'! Many candidates had no idea what a fraction was and could not turn a simple fraction into a decimal even when it was explained to them. Six out of every seven candidates were failing the entrance tests, not so much from lack of ability as from inadequate teaching. Charles decided to alter his entrance tests to accommodate these children, and within two years of admitting them to his schools he found that they were well up to what he regarded as acceptable standards of academic achievement.

He had no time for the 'free expression' methods of English teaching which were fashionable from the 1960s onwards. It had been decided in some influential educational circles that as long as a child was expressing something of his own personality and imagination, such things as grammar, spelling and punctuation were relatively unimportant. The pages of 'creative writing' thus produced might well be unintelligible to anyone who assumed that English was written in sentences which began with a capital letter and ended with a full stop, but the child could earn high praise from his teacher if the piece was written 'from the heart'.

Such a teacher would not, of course, be welcome at an Oxley school. Charles would scrutinise, with red pen literally in hand, any application for a teaching post. If the applicant did not write in cursive (joined up) script or there was any untidiness or even slight illegibility, a large red cross appeared on the front of the application form. Spelling mistakes earned the perpetrator an equally dismissive response.

'I don't care how well qualified they are, what their experience has been or what wonderful human beings they are,' he said. 'If they can't write and spell properly, I won't have them.'

Union activists rarely even tried to step over the threshold of Oxley terrain, although he knew that some of his teachers were members of unions and he understood their reasons for membership. What he objected to was the way that unions had led the trend towards an education *industry* and away from the teaching *profession*. The union he had most time and respect for was the Professional Association of Teachers, not least because of their no-strike policy. One of his staff at Hamilton College was an executive committee member of PAT, whose General Secretary, Peter Dawson, was a visitor more than once to Hamilton and a Speech Day guest speaker at Scarisbrick Hall.

Once Tower College was firmly established as a school where the pupils looked smart, worked hard, behaved politely and achieved academic success, the drive continued to achieve better and better results in GCE Ordinary Level examinations. Without a Sixth Form, the school had 'O' Levels as its ultimate yardstick for Charles' pupils. He would encourage them to attempt as many subjects as possible, even if they had to study some of them outside the school timetable.

Totals of 12, 13 or even 14 subject passes became the targets regularly achieved and triumphantly announced in the local papers.

Charles always looked for opportunities to get some good 'publickity' (a pronunciation he borrowed from Muriel's father) for his schools; he made sure that the Press had invitations to Speech Days, at which he would not only outline the achievements of his pupils but also express strong opinions on some matter of educational controversy.

At a sports day for the Independent Schools Association, Charles and Muriel accompanied by both their mothers and a stroppy-looking Rachel (who clearly enjoyed wearing her school hat and is now Principal of Tower College!).

He angered the headteachers of some state schools in St Helens over the publication of GCE results. When the Government and the Exam Boards agreed to abandon the Pass/Fail dividing line and to award certificates for grades below the former Pass mark, Charles refused to go along with the change, believing, as did many others, that it was designed to lower standards. Therefore, when he sent the Tower College 'O' Level results to the local newspaper, he stressed that they included only A, B and C grades, which were equivalent to the former Pass standard. He suspected that some or all of the state schools in the area submitted results which included the lower grades as well. He wrote to the paper and to the heads of all the local secondary schools to try to reach uniformity, but without success. The newspaper would print only what the schools sent them and some of the heads were reluctant to risk adverse comparison with an independent school.

Charles wanted everybody to understand exactly what was expected of them if they worked in, or sent their children to, one of his schools; so he produced a Parents' Guide, a Staff Handbook and a Pupils' Guide. Each booklet spelt out in considerable detail the school's—i.e. *his*—expectations. The Pupils' Guide also provided plenty of material for naughty children to write out neatly as a punishment.

In the Staff Handbook, after sections on the school's background, general policy, Christian character and staff organisation, a page headed 'Members of Staff' specified: 'To accept an appointment as a staff member is to undertake an obligation to maintain appropriate standards of dress and deportment. Gentlemen wear jacket, collar and tie; ladies do not wear trousers. Smoking and drinking are not allowed on the school premises.'

By maintaining high standards themselves, teachers could then command the respect of pupils. 'Staff members must insist that all pupils address them properly, gentlemen as "Sir", ladies by name, "Miss or Mrs ..." "Ms" is not used. Pupils must be made to stand properly when addressing or being addressed by a staff member. Undue familiarity must be discouraged.'

To Charles, such beliefs were grounded not in chauvinism or sexism. Starting from the New Testament view that men should look manly and women feminine, he regarded the sexes as equal but different; women who wore trousers and used the label 'Ms' were deliberately or ignorantly blurring divinely created distinctions. *Vive la différence* might also have been his watchword when it came to school uniform. For he required girls to wear a school hat or beret throughout their school lives—even in Sixth Form—whereas boys could dispense with their school cap at the end of Year 9, the third year of Senior School. Originally, the stipulation for boys had been that they must wear a cap until they attained the height of five feet ten inches, but he was eventually persuaded that for some, this amounted to a life sentence!

Charles and Muriel had worked hard to see Tower College well established both as a school and as a business, but they knew that official recognition by the Ministry of Education was all-important for the status of an independent school. Charles therefore applied to the Ministry, who duly sent along a team of inspectors to observe at close quarters every aspect of the running of the school. As brisk and outwardly confident as ever, he betrayed no sign of any qualms he might be feeling as he awaited the outcome of the inspection. All seemed to go well and when the report arrived it was favourable, so now the Oxleys could advertise their school with the Government's seal of approval—'recognised as efficient by the Ministry of Education'.

All four of their own children were now growing up through the Kindergarten, Junior and Senior departments of Tower College. In addition to his school and family responsibilities, Charles was fully involved in the preaching and ministry of Brethren assemblies all round Merseyside and South-West Lancashire. His vast knowledge of the biblical text and languages had been a key factor in his B A Honours degree in Biblical and Classical Studies at the University of Liverpool. What he also needed if he was to be an effective preacher was the application of that knowledge to the needs of fellow-believers, so that by prayer, faith and the operation of the Holy Spirit they could be challenged and equipped to live the Christian life. Those who heard him speak from pulpit and platform recognised that his words came not just from the head but from the heart as well.

Now that Tower College was well established, Charles found at different times that Christian parents were asking whether he would consider taking boarders. Although the premises were unsuitable, he and Muriel did not totally dismiss the concerns of missionary families and other expatriates who wanted to be able to place their offspring in a Christian boarding school with high academic and disciplinary standards. Local education authorities were open in those days to the possibility of giving grants for the children of expatriates to take up boarding school places.

Nevertheless, if God wanted Charles and Muriel Oxley to open another school with boarders in mind, they needed very clear guidance, preferably with numerous confirming signs!

It was therefore in a spirit of only mild curiosity that they drove across south-west Lancashire, one day in 1963, to have a look at Scarisbrick Hall. As thrifty business people, they were always

Reputedly the finest example of residential neo-gothic architecture in England, the main building of Scarisbrick Hall School, established in 1964. The school amalgamated and became 'Kingswood College at Scarisbrick Hall' in 1998.

on the lookout for sales of carpets, furniture or books, and as the teacher training college which had been occupying the Hall had now moved to amalgamate with another college in Liverpool, there might be bargains.

Scarisbrick Hall is a 150-room mansion set in 440 acres halfway between the small market town of Ormskirk and the Lancashire coastal resort of Southport. The history of the Hall dates back to 1238, when the wooded estate passed from an owner blessed with the name of Simon de Grubhead to his brother, Gilbert de Scarisbrick. He was the first in a long line of Scarisbricks; one of his descendants was knighted on the battlefield at Agincourt. In 1595 a twenty-room half-timbered Elizabethan house was built by Edward Scarisbrick, a royalist, from whom the estate was confiscated in 1599. It was returned to his son James, who, like his four Jesuit brothers, was an ardent supporter of Charles II. Some adherents of the Old Pretender, including the Duke of Norfolk, met at Scarisbrick Hall in 1732 to discuss a Jacobite plot, and at least two Scarisbricks took part in the 1745 rebellion.

In 1833 the estate was inherited by Charles Scarisbrick, who commissioned Augustus Pugin to spare no expense in building a new mansion in stone on the site of the old dwelling. During the time he was working on Scarisbrick Hall, Pugin was also collaborating with Sir Charles Barry on the new Houses of Parliament, and the tower which houses Big Ben is said to have been modelled on the 170-foot tower at Scarisbrick. Charles Scarisbrick collected paintings and beautiful oak carvings from Venice and from the cathedrals of Rouen and Antwerp to decorate the Hall, which is said to be the finest example of neo-Gothic residential architecture in England.

Charles Scarisbrick died before the building work was completed, leaving over three million pounds to his widowed sister, Lady Ann. She devoted her considerable energies, with the help of the younger Pugin, Edward, to finishing the hall and gardens in grandiose style. Then, on her death, the estate passed to her daughter, the Marquise de Casteja, but, after gambling debts had reduced the family fortunes, the Hall was sold to another branch of the family.

During the Second World War Scarisbrick Hall passed out of private ownership and became a Red Cross convalescent home. Then, in 1946, the Church of England Commissioners bought it to set up a teacher training college. With the help of grants, £250,000 was spent in putting the building into a sound structural condition and equipping the Hall as a modern college. Playing fields and tennis courts were laid out, new buildings erected to provide a gymnasium, a dining hall, a chapel and additional bedroom accommodation. Central heating and modern kitchen equipment were installed.

The Robbins Report on Higher Education, published in 1963, recommended that training colleges of 200 students were uneconomical on teaching staff. In July of that year St Katherine's College vacated the premises at Scarisbrick Hall for the move to Liverpool, becoming part of the Liverpool Institute for Higher Education and latterly Liverpool Hope University College.

The Scarisbrick estate was quickly snapped up by a property company intent on prestigious housing, but the County Planning Authority declared the Hall to be a building of outstanding architectural and historic value and made a preservation order on the whole estate, thereby preventing any development. The property company, now anxious to sell, advertised the Hall and grounds for sale.

Charles and Muriel were impressed from the moment that they turned from the Southport-Ormskirk main road into the splendid, tree-lined, half-mile drive up to the Hall. As they looked round the magnificent main building and the additional modern facilities, they both knew it would be an ideal place for a Christian boarding school. They felt God was making very clear signals to them: it was clear that there was a demand for such a school and that Scarisbrick Hall was suitable to meet that need; they had amassed fifteen years' experience of running a school at Tower College; Charles was just into his 40s and Muriel nearing hers, both in good fettle and lacking neither energy nor enthusiasm. Two factors were crucial—the cost, of course, since their funds were limited; and the timing of events, because Charles had accepted an invitation to go to India for the opening of Delhi Bible Institute. It was not in his nature to sit and wait for his prayers to be answered, so he began to push a few doors to see which stayed open and which were slammed shut.

His first move was to persuade the property company to divide up the estate so that the Hall and 38 acres comprised one lot for auction. This area included the playing fields, the gardens, the lake and the main drive, but left out the extensive farmlands around the rest of the estate. The central lot was then put up for sale by public auction by Messrs. Jackson-Stopps and Staff of Chester on Monday 30th September 1963.

Arriving at the Hall on the day of the auction, Charles and Muriel made a few astute enquiries to find out the nature of the opposition. The Home Office had thoughts of setting up an 'approved school' for young offenders; a group of hoteliers from Manchester saw the potential for a country club; and the representative of a well-known holiday camp company was also present.

The large drawing-room was packed as the auctioneer announced the details of the lot and then started the bidding at £10,000.

£15,000 ... £17,500 ... Surely it would go much higher than this, to a point some way beyond the Oxleys' upper limit? £20,000 ... £22,000 ... £24,000 ... £24,500 ... The bidding stopped! The lot was withdrawn.

Charles and Muriel were convinced that God was holding doors open for them. Charles knew that he had an advantage over other interested parties in that he would not need planning permission for change of use from a teacher training college to a boarding school. He immediately started negotiations and, after several anxious but exhilarating days, he managed to convince the property company that they would be well advised to settle for the proverbial bird in the hand.

A few hours before his plane took off for India, the owners accepted his offer of £24,500 and contracts were signed. It was, as he himself described it, 'the bargain of the century.'

The valuable oak carvings, statues and paintings were offered to Charles for a further £5,500 but he declined. At a further auction in November they realised over £16,000, but planning permission for their removal from the Hall was refused, so that most of the carvings and some of the paintings remain there to this day. When an insurance company came to assess the Hall and its contents, they would not insure it for anything less than a quarter of a million pounds ... and that was in 1963.

Once the purchase was completed, Muriel's skills and experience came to the fore. She set to work arranging for the entire redecoration and furnishing of the 150 rooms while her husband was busy recruiting staff, interviewing parents, enrolling pupils and setting up the organisation of the new school. In the following twelve months, over a thousand rolls of wallpaper were hung, several hundred gallons of paint were applied, many tons of furniture installed in bedrooms, classrooms and common rooms, and the chapel, dining hall and science laboratories were fitted out. All this, of course, was in addition to the daily running of Tower College.

On 12th September 1964 Scarisbrick Hall School opened with 84 boys, 25 of whom were boarders. At the opening ceremony in a packed school chapel, Dr W J Martin of the University of Liverpool gave a stirring address to the boys, their parents and the staff, and Professor F F Bruce, one of the giants of biblical scholarship, from the University of Manchester, led the company in a prayer that the school would be used for the glory of God in the service of the Lord Jesus Christ.

Initially the school catered mainly for the secondary age range, with just a handful of boys under eleven, but as numbers increased, so did the demand for the full Junior School age range to give continuity right through from the age of seven to A Levels. When two girls' independent schools in Southport closed down in the early 1970s, parents pleaded with Charles to admit girls at Scarisbrick, particularly those whose daughters could then join their brothers who were already there. Although some of the staff had misgivings about the change and some of the facilities were not best suited to a mixed school, it was nonetheless the right move to make. A few years later, Charles began also to admit girls as boarders, some time before the trend for single-sex public schools to become at least partially coeducational. Then, as academic standards of children taking the entrance tests continued to fall, Charles opened a Kindergarten (Infants) department so that children from the age of four could benefit from a Scarisbrick education throughout their school lives.

Tower College's catchment area was mainly industrial—St Helens, Warrington, Widnes, the eastern fringes of Liverpool—but Scarisbrick Hall School cast its net over a more diverse area. The social and geographical mix showed itself in the variety of accents to be heard among the pupils: cosmopolitan sophistication rubbed shoulders with Lancastrian farming folk, while hard-headed Wiganers mixed with sharp-witted Scousers. The boarding element, which peaked at 130 pupils, added an international flavour from Africa, India, the Middle East and Hong Kong in particular. Chinese boarders were almost monastic in their devotion to study, even in leisure time; rising at 5 a.m., working until midnight, relaxing only rarely with a game of table tennis or an illicit boiling of rice for a midnight feast. One Malaysian's understanding of practical Physics increased considerably when he placed his large frame into a full bath of water; the overflow surprised not only himself but also resident staff in the room immediately below!

Although his home base was still Tower College, Charles took his share of residential duties among the boarders at Scarisbrick, usually one or two evenings plus as much of the weekend as he could fit in. He insisted that Sunday should be a different day from any other (one which many pupils found tedious): all boarders must attend a church service in the morning, according to their parents' denominational preference, and in the afternoon he would run a Bible class. There was to be no televiewing on Sundays. Even during the week, the large television in the boarders' common room could only be switched on for certain approved programmes.

In addition to its large number of rooms, Scarisbrick Hall has extensive cellars, which were known to attract adventurous boarders from time to time. One night when Charles was working late in his ground-floor study, he became aware of voices moving about below his feet. He stopped and listened.

'I don't think we've been here before, have we?' said one voice.

'Don't think so,' said another. 'Any idea where we are?'

Grinning to himself, Charles could not resist joining in. 'You're directly under my study and you'd better get up here as quickly as possible!' Feet scuttled, mouse-like, away through the cellars and a minute or two later a couple of dishevelled and downcast boys duly appeared to receive their reprimand.

Charles kept the boarders on a tight rein, partly because of his own principles and upbringing, partly because he had seen the value of a strict regime during his time in Egypt. He tried to apply the Mikado's dictum of letting the punishment fit the crime, so the range of sanctions included essay-writing, loss of privileges, being 'gated' (not allowed out at weekends except to go to church) and the slipper. 'Strict but fair' is the verdict of many of his former pupils, though he clearly got it wrong at times.

An Irish boy, John Gilmore, had a wicked smile, remarkable consistency in finding himself in trouble and no sign of a grudge when caught and punished. One day he happened to notice that a fire hose had been partially pulled off its reel on the wall in a corridor and turned on, because there was a noticeable puddle on the woodblock floor. He turned off the hose and was winding it back on to its reel when Charles appeared round the corner, saw the puddle, the hose and the Irish scallywag and sent him straight to the headmaster's study. On arriving there himself, Charles administered the slipper swiftly and firmly.

'Well, Gilmore, what have you to say for yourself?'

'Sir, I know what you saw and I can understand why you thought I must be responsible, but honestly, sir, it wasn't me. I was actually putting the hose back when you found me.'

'All right, Gilmore, I believe you're honest. I apologise for punishing you without first hearing your version of events. Let's say that this punishment covers all those occasions when you've been up to something and not been caught, shall we?'

'Fair enough, sir.'

Charles Oxley refused to sanction the formation of parent-teacher organisations in his schools. Ignoring the significant reservoir of goodwill that might have been tapped, he insisted that the roles of parents and teachers were complementary but separate. The parents' job was to pay fees promptly and make sure that their offspring put in full attendance, did their homework properly and maintained smart appearance. (He carried out weekly hair checks for the boys: it must be 'off the ears and off the collar.') He regarded PTA's as excuses for wine-bibbing and socialising—he was staunchly teetotal—and for raising funds for the school. The businessman in him rejected the latter because, if a school was to be successful, it must make the grade as a business as well as educationally.

He formed a company, Christian Schools Limited, to run Tower College and Scarisbrick Hall. As Principal and Bursar respectively, he and Muriel would receive a salary, just like any member of the teaching staff. The company was to be non-profit-making, so that any excess of fees income over expenditure must be used for the benefit of the school. Coming from families which had built up successful businesses, both Charles and Muriel knew the value of thrift and made every effort to eliminate waste in the running of the schools. They kept the fees as low as possible in order to encourage the not-so-well-off parents who, with some self-sacrifice, could manage to provide an independent school education for their children.

Charles was not averse to receiving gifts, however, and when the school had been running for barely a year, Sir John and Lady Laing handed him a cheque for £5,000, a handsome amount in 1965. Head of the large construction company, Sir John told Charles he had been praying for over twenty years that God would raise up an evangelical boarding school in the North of England and he was delighted to find that his prayers had been answered in Scarisbrick Hall School.

Chapter 5

BATTLES WITH BROADCASTERS

Most people have at some time or other thought of writing to complain about a television programme they have seen; only a small proportion of them have actually done so. Few, if any, will have written as frequently and persistently as Charles Oxley. A cursory check through his correspondence files after his death revealed many bulging folders of such letters. As with all his letters, he always kept a carbon copy of what he had written and then clipped to it whatever reply he received. In correspondence with broadcasting companies he often felt the need to follow up his original letter, as he was rarely satisfied with the 'polite brush-off' reply he felt he normally received.

Instances of blasphemy, swearing and vulgarity most often had Charles reaching for his typewriter to remind the broadcasting authorities of their duty not to offend against good taste or decency. Inevitably the broadcasters' replies claimed that they were merely reflecting the language and attitudes prevalent in much of society; to which Charles would say that the media were in fact setting the standards which society adopted.

He would not settle for a bland reply from somebody's secretary or even the self-justification of the producer of the offending programme. It was those in charge of programme scheduling that he sought to confront and convince, so his letters often went to the Director-General of the BBC or the controller of a particular channel or the Chairman of the IBA.

Not all of his letters were critical or complaining. In December 1973 he wrote to congratulate the producer of Radio 2's *Your Hundred Best Tunes* on what he regarded as 'the best radio programme of the week', with its 'superb choice of music for Sunday evening listening' and the 'gentle, almost reverent way in which Alan Keith introduces the pieces.'

An exchange of letters lasting four and a half months arose out of three words spoken by a Radio 4 announcer at 7.45 a.m. one morning in April 1978. Charles had heard the voice say, '*According to legend*, Hiram, King of Tyre, helped Solomon in the building of the Temple.' His immediate telephone call to Broadcasting House asking for a correction to be broadcast was unsuccessful, so he followed with a letter of complaint about the use of the word 'legend' in reference to part of the scriptures sacred to both the Jewish and Christian faiths. The Senior Assistant in the BBC Secretariat, to whom Charles' letter came, had no inkling of how doggedly determined this particular listener would turn out to be!

Charles went to the trouble of quoting nine eminent biblical scholars to support his point that Hiram's co-operation with Solomon was historical fact and not legend. As a Bible scholar and teacher himself, this was more than just an intellectual disagreement. As he put it in one of the letters, 'You may think I am making a fuss over a minor academic inaccuracy. I am not. I am trying to express a deep sense of outrage that those now in charge of the nation's broadcasting service, which I held in such high personal regard before and during the war, are so insensitive as to persist in describing as "legend" a biblical passage which is well authenticated by archaeology and contemporary historical records, and in so doing show contempt for what I and many others hold most dear—our faith in the Holy Scriptures as the Word of God.'

One letter from a BBC official did give Charles a pleasant surprise. He had been listening to Radio 4 one morning and heard a 'trail' for a play later in the day, containing language hardly suited to breakfast-time listening for many families. He wrote to complain. The reply from the Presentation Editor of Radio 4 agreed that such language should not be used in a morning 'trail' for an adult play to be broadcast in the evening. He apologised and promised to take action to ensure there would be no repetition: 'I think we have a duty not to thrust what may be offensive upon the unsuspecting listener.'

Charles was so thrilled at such a positive response that he wrote back to express his gratitude: 'I have been writing to the BBC for over twenty years, usually, I am afraid, to complain, but occasionally to congratulate, and I can say that your letter is the most encouraging reply I have ever received from any member of the BBC. I wish you every success in your efforts to curb the use of bad language.'

Charles himself made many contributions to the media over the years. He knew the value of keeping the press informed of news items which could give good publicity to the schools, and he frequently wrote letters to editors to give a Christian slant on some topical issue. He became well known for his outspoken remarks on matters of moral concern and news editors would ring and ask for his comments when a story was likely to cause controversy.

He cultivated his contacts with reporters on national newspapers also, and they too came to regard him as a good man for a pertinent quote in areas where Christian standards were threatened. The two local radio stations nearest to his St Helens home—Radio Merseyside and Radio City—often drew on his wide knowledge and unequivocal stance for interviews and discussion programmes. He took the trouble to find out Radio Merseyside's requirements for their *Thought for the Day* and sent in some scripts for their approval. The outcome was the opportunity to present uplifting, Bible-based three-minute talks on five consecutive weekday mornings.

Charles' initiative brought him a regular job with South Lancashire Newspapers, the group which included the St Helens Reporter among its publications. In August 1975 he wrote to the editor suggesting that there was room for a weekly column to give a Christian comment on a topical issue. He backed up his suggestion with two samples, offering to do the job himself without payment. The Group Editor's reply was prompt and pleasing: 'You have just acquired a new job! The two samples you enclosed hit exactly the right note.'

So began *This and That* by Jonathan Hope, a pseudonym Charles insisted on maintaining in order that he could be free to make comments without having them linked in people's minds with the principal of a local independent school. He had the happy knack of picking out an item of news which would either outrage, amuse or sadden most people, then use humour or a pertinent illustration to apply some Christian principle without preaching at his readers.

In his role as Jonathan Hope he once found himself in a fascinating correspondence with one of his Tower College pupils. Nathanael Wright, aged eleven, showed such a flair for writing and such a strong Christian faith that Charles, alias Jonathan, suggested that he might take over the column when he himself was too old. Nathanael, however, was intent on being a missionary doctor and regretted that he might not be able to send an article to St Helens every week from wherever in the world he might be working. He did put forward the name of his younger brother who he felt could do the job just as well. Anyway, wrote Nathanael, when the time came for Jonathan Hope to retire, he would be the special guest at a party to be given by Nathanael's mother! In the meantime, he hoped that after his years at Tower College, 'an independent school where the headmaster Mr Oxley is a Christian,' he would go as a boarder to Mr Oxley's other school, Scarisbrick Hall, which he knew had beautiful grounds and two swans on the lake.

To see young Christians taking their stand in such enterprising ways delighted Charles, who was always looking for ways to channel their enthusiasm profitably. In 1975 he suggested to some of the senior boarders at Scarisbrick Hall a project which was to arouse keen interest nationwide.

Blasphemy, swearing and vulgarity on radio and television were guaranteed to raise Charles' hackles and stir him to yet another letter of complaint. But would the BBC and IBA be able to apply the polite brush-off to a large-scale survey of their output? Michael Hastings, who later became a television presenter himself, was a 17 year old Christian from the Caribbean; Charles asked him to chair a team of twenty-three boarders aged between 15 and 19. They came from a variety of racial, religious, cultural and domestic backgrounds, so that nobody could accuse them of being stereotypical in their upbringing and attitudes.

The task that Charles invited them to undertake was to watch, between them, every minute of every programme on BBC1 and ITV from the early evening news until closedown for a whole week. (This was in the days before programmes continued throughout the night and before the days of Channels 4 and 5; otherwise they might have needed a team three times as large!) From the total of more than eighty hours of viewing the team of monitors would make notes during each programme and write up a report afterwards. The monitors would then hold a series of discussions based on their findings and produce a final report.

The Hastings Report found that news programmes concentrated mainly on unpleasant aspects of life—wars, strikes, crime and protests—but it recognised that people needed to be informed of events such as the massacre of thousands of people in Vietnam and Cambodia. The chief news monitor confessed that by the end of the week he was feeling 'depressed and pessimistic.'

Sports coverage received high commendation, but the best overall rating was given to documentaries, which the monitors found 'more enjoyable than programmes which set out to entertain.' Much of the week's drama output earned the comment 'heartily disliked' because of confused plots, bad-tempered and humourless characters, and an over-indulgence of swearing and blasphemy. A Sunday evening play amassed fifteen blasphemies and forty-three swear words in an hour. *Play for Today* won the title of worst programme of the whole week; it 'lacked real dramatic quality and relied heavily on offensive dialogue for any semblance of realism.' The obscenities in the play came so frequently that monitors reckoned to have logged only about 80% of them. One boy found the language at first shocking, then boring; another felt 'disgust at first, then anger.'

The whole of that Thursday evening's viewing (which included the play) came in for scathing criticism, with the exception of *Top of the Pops* and a half-hour documentary on faith healing. For the rest, the BBC offered 'a continuous stream of vulgarity, swearing and blasphemy during peak viewing time, i.e. from 8 p.m. until 10.40'; on ITV, apart from the documentary, 'objectionable and offensive material broadcast from 7.05 until 12.20.'

Only when reports on individual programmes were collated did the monitoring team realise just how much swearing, vulgarity and blasphemy they had witnessed. Attempts to record all instances must err on the low side, but they did note eighty-four instances of blasphemy, one hundred and fifteen of vulgarity and two hundred and seven of swearing, in various types of programmes and at all times of the evening through the week.

Commercial advertising brought a mixture of amusement and irritation, but the report highlighted the fact that, on the Saturday evening, fourteen advertisements for alcoholic drink appeared in six hours twenty minutes. A separate paragraph of the report drew attention to the indirect advertising of alcohol:—

> Drinking beer or more often spirits was frequently shown on very many programmes, as though it were normal for people to be drinking all the time at home and in hotels. In the discussion group it was felt that the portrayal of drinking to this extent as a normal domestic activity has in fact increased its acceptance as normal conduct and will continue to do so. It was believed that this indirect advertising was done deliberately. Some thought the same to be true of cigar and cigarette smoking.

The Hastings Report was aimed primarily at the BBC and IBA, but Charles was shrewd enough to realise that the press and public opinion would quickly respond to it. Michael Hastings was interviewed on radio and television as well as by the press. A mass of letters flooded in from all over the country. When Michael went home to the West Indies in the school holidays, Charles had to deal with correspondence and enquiries himself.

Six months after the first report, the monitoring team decided to do a follow-up, this time to draw comparisons and see whether there had been any significant reduction in the amount of swearing, blasphemy and vulgarity being beamed into the nation's homes. Although they were pleased to find that blasphemy and swearing had been reduced, the amount of vulgarity, particularly in comedy programmes, had risen significantly.

On two occasions Charles arranged meetings for representatives of the IBA to answer questions about television standards. At one of them, in a Southport hotel, with about 200 people present, the Regional Officer for the North-West, whose job was to see that Granada Television kept within the requirements of the Independent Television Act, tried to play down any link between violence on television and in real life. He referred to the Belson Report and said that it spoke only of a 'possible link.' Charles, however, had come prepared with Mary Whitehouse's article *The Corruption of Culture*, in which she quoted the actual wording of the report: the evidence was 'very strongly supportive' of a connection between violence seen on TV and violence actually committed.

The other IBA official present at this meeting dismissed the suggestion that programmes such as *The Sweeney* showed the police in a poor light and claimed that the police enjoyed such programmes. Charles again had his ammunition at the ready—a news cutting in which a Chief Constable had complained about television's portrayal of the police and the Secretary of the Prison Officers' Association had expressed equal annoyance at the way prison officers were presented on TV.

In his capacity as chairman of the meeting Charles had the chance to sum up. In thanking the IBA officials for attending, he reminded them that many people felt deeply concerned about the amount of blasphemy, violence and vulgarity, the lack of quality in drama, comedy and light entertainment, and the unwillingness of the BBC and the IBA to change their policy of giving the public the programmes they liked to watch, even at the risk of offending sizeable numbers of viewers. Charles urged that broadcasting should come under the Obscene Publications Act, that there should be a Consumer Council for Broadcasting and that the annual reports of the BBC and IBA should be subjected to parliamentary debates.

Charles and Muriel with another redoubtable campaigner, Mary Whitehouse, of the National Viewers and Listeners Association, in 1976.

At public meetings of this kind Charles always took the opportunity to promote the work of the National Viewers and Listeners Association. His first link with NVALA came early in 1974 when he wrote to ask for information about its 10th Anniversary Convention. The letter of reply, giving full details, was signed 'E.R. Whitehouse', and when Charles later wrote to express regret that a full diary prevented him from attending the Convention, he did not know that the signature was that of Mary's husband Ernest, so he addressed his letter to 'Mr/Mrs/Miss E.R. Whitehouse'. It was not long, however, before Charles was in the front rank of Mary Whitehouse's allies, so much so that she invited him to become National Vice-President of NVALA as well as co-ordinating the work in the North-West and Midlands.

The perpetual problem for Charles was that although he had the will and the energy to undertake such new commitments, he never had enough hours in the day. In October 1979 he wrote to Mrs Whitehouse after writing a review of one of her books:

> The reading of the book has made me feel even more aware of the importance of your work and the need for its continuance. I would very much like to play a part in the ongoing campaign and regard it as a great honour to be asked to play a leading part. Only one thing holds me back and that is I would have to relinquish a considerable amount of work I am doing at present. There are several commitments I could give up to others without much difficulty, and I am thinking how I can free myself. I am praying for the Lord's guidance in this matter, as you are, and will take an early opportunity of discussing it with you.

One of the most publicised campaigns of NVALA concerned the film *The Life of Brian*, in which the Monty Python team were seen to be mocking the person of Jesus Christ and the biblical record of his life, miracles and resurrection. Attempts by Christians to prevent the film being shown in their localities were unsuccessful, so Charles and others decided on a different strategy. They had hundreds of pamphlets printed in which a clear warning was given about its blasphemous content and the distortions it used in order to poke fun at the Lord Jesus. Teams of volunteers formed silent vigils outside cinemas where the film was showing, some giving out the pamphlets to the queuing public, others holding placards of protest. They were able to engage in some useful conversations about the reality of Jesus and the truth of gospel accounts of his life.

Evangelical Christians have been complaining for years about the liberal-humanist monopoly in the broadcasting media which has either marginalised or trivialised Biblical Christianity. No doubt the excesses and moral weaknesses of some American televangelists have made programmers and politicians on this side of the Atlantic cautious about opening up the airwaves to evangelicals or charismatics, some of whom would make good use of television time if given the chance.

In April 1984 Channel 4 presented a programme called *Jesus—the Evidence*, a title suggesting a balanced investigation of the historical facts about Jesus Christ. It turned out to be a heavily biased attack on the Gospel narratives and, in an hour-long programme, the one conservative scholar had just a few seconds allotted to him. Charles watched the programme with rising anger. He immediately telephoned Channel 4's London headquarters to register a strong complaint with the duty officer. He followed up with a scathing attack on those responsible for such a one-sided programme, using his Liverpool Bible College notepaper to add weight to his letter of complaint.

It seems that many other people also complained, for two weeks later Channel 4's Commissioning Editor replied: 'The substantial objection that the series obscured significant evidence by omission has prompted Channel 4 to screen a one-hour follow-up discussion programme.' It was to be called *Jesus: Fact and Faith* and would call on various biblical scholars to present their case. All credit to the television company for not ignoring a strong body of public protest and for mounting the second programme; the only problem for Charles and others was that it was screened early on a Sunday evening, when many could not watch because of their church commitments.

The same Channel 4 earned no credit at all, however, when in 1987 its programme controllers rejected a series entitled *Jesus—Then and Now* in which the renowned Anglican evangelical Rev. David Watson gave a balanced presentation of the central truths of the Christian faith. Channel 4 refused to show it on the grounds that it was 'propagandist' (are not most of the Channel's more serious programmes?) and of 'poor quality'. Yet a year before, an adapted version of the series had been screened on Welsh Channel 4 and was consistently in the top ten most watched programmes. With additional filming and editing, the series would certainly have commanded decent audiences. It had the support of many church groups, including Roman Catholics, and its rejection appeared to confirm the view of Charles and other Christians that the only kind of Christianity likely to be broadcast was a wishy-washy liberalism.

Charles' letter to Jeremy Isaacs, then Chief Executive of Channel 4, stated that he was 'dismayed though not altogether surprised to read that Channel Four has rejected the series *Jesus—Then and Now*. Films of the most degrading type, with obscene language and explicit sex and violence are shown incessantly *ad nauseam*. When a really decent film is offered, it is rejected.'

The same Mr Isaacs received another letter from Charles when Channel 4 used the device of a red warning triangle on the screen to enable them to show outrageous films with apparent impunity. *The Life and Loves of a She Devil* contained blasphemy, vulgarity, nudity, sexual perversion, violence and reference to the occult—'everything to which I object,' wrote Charles. 'As a schoolmaster, I know that school children, some of them quite young, have television sets in their bedrooms and they watch the obscene films which you broadcast and are morally damaged as a result. I know that parents should exercise greater control, but some parents are out working, others are one-parent families. The inadequacies of some parents are no excuse for your Authority to issue such poisonous materials into people's homes. Broadcasting generally has, I believe, reached an all-time low and Channel 4 is at the bottom.' (Channel 5 did not appear until after Charles' death!)

He was quite convinced that if Jesus had lived in the latter half of the twentieth century he would have made use whenever possible of the broadcasting media to proclaim the kingdom of God. Likewise John Wesley might have been spared some of the quarter of a million miles he rode on horseback to preach the gospel had there been television channels available to him. What Billy Graham and others have achieved in the USA has yet to happen in the UK—to convince programme controllers that there is a place for authentic vibrant Christianity somewhere in the terrestrial schedules. *Songs of Praise* caters for lovers of Christian hymns and songs, with some worthwhile testimonies thrown in, but apart from an occasional documentary about, for example, Jackie Pullinger's work in the Walled City of Hong Kong, nobody would be able to find out from television just what God is doing in the world at large.

In the 1970s Charles was thinking in terms of a Christian magazine programme or even a Bible quiz show, which he believed could be both entertaining and informative, and certainly no worse than some of the other game shows that have been foisted upon innocent viewers in recent decades! He also had a friend, Ernest McQuoid, who had presented a twenty-minute Christian programme immediately after *News at Ten* on Ulster Television and had been lined up to do a Christian magazine series, including a quiz, until the station's budgets had been slashed and the plans had to be shelved.

In the summer of 1986 Charles contacted Ernest, a genial Irishman who was Chief Welfare Officer for British Telecom, to share his thoughts. 'Regarding the format: when I first had the idea a few years ago, I put a suggested format down in the "Ideas" section of my loose leaf notebook. I enclose a photocopy of what I wrote. It was not intended to be read by anyone but myself, so please excuse the tiny writing. I tend to write such things during dreary sermons, with frequent glances at the speaker who gets the impression that I am gratefully making notes on his address!' As to the level at which the quiz should be pitched? 'The level of seriousness could be about that of *Top of the Form* or *My Music*. *Brain of Britain* is too high-powered and that Transatlantic Quiz programme is so pretentious as to be a pain in the neck. No doubt there will be some dear brethren (and others) who would feel such a programme to be irreverent, but I think there is full justification for a programme which chooses questions that contain Biblical truth and which presents that truth in a pleasant and sometimes humorous manner.'

Both Charles and Ernest were realistic enough to know that their greatest problem would be to convince the broadcasting authorities that there would be sufficient interest in such a programme. Perhaps a single pilot programme would be able to test the response.

Charles had a contact at Yorkshire Television who gave enthusiastic support, had him meet the company's Head of Religious Broadcasting and urged him to prepare a pilot programme. Charles did so, only to find two months later that the television company could not find a slot in their schedules for this kind of programme.

One idea of his that did materialise was a programme in the BBC1 series, *Choices*. He felt that many people, including Christians, misunderstood the biblical basis of forgiveness. In an age where tolerance was increasingly becoming a supreme virtue, often at the expense of justice, he saw the need to re-emphasise repentance as the prerequisite of forgiveness. He put forward the suggestion to the BBC after having previously appeared on two of the *Choices* programmes as a participating member of the audience. On this occasion also he had his chance to speak, but he was disappointed that the essential point was lost among a variety of voices, each opinion being given equal validity whether or not it had a sure foundation of truth.

The BBC Radio programme *Any Questions* always provokes lively discussion among the invited members of the panel and among those who respond in *Any Answers*. In October 1980 Charles succeeded in not only having a letter read out on *Any Answers* but also dealing succinctly with two questions where he felt biblical truth had been ignored:—

> In their reply to the question on the ordination of women in the Church of England, not one of your panellists referred to the Biblical prohibition, which has been observed by the Church for centuries, but presumptuously decided the issue in their own 'wisdom' on the basis of expediency.
>
> If Jesus Christ is the Head of the Church and if it is the Church of the Lord Jesus Christ, then surely it is *His* rules that must prevail and not the pressures of a permissive society.

Chapter 6

SEX SHOPS AND BLASPHEMY

In July 1977 the Home Secretary, Merlyn Rees, appointed a committee under the chairmanship of Professor Bernard Williams to look at the Obscene Publications Act of 1959 and try to remove its confusion and ineffectiveness. The specific area it would consider was 'Obscenity and Film Censorship', but when Charles Oxley saw the names of those chosen to serve on the committee, he was convinced that they would promote a 'permissive humanist view' of the subject.

He had grown up in a society where the public had had limited access to pornographic material, partly because of censorship laws and partly because most ordinary people were disgusted by pornography. In his view, however, 'the retreat from Christian standards of morality since the war has changed all that. The demand for pornographic material has grown in volume astronomically and has developed in intensity from so-called "soft porn" to "hard porn"—naked men and women engaged in disgusting sexual perversions, more recently involving children and animals.'

He was concerned about the addictive power of pornography and the way in which, as with drug addiction, the desire for something successively stronger could dominate a vulnerable mind. Pornography was best defined for him by the Longford Report as 'material deliberately designed to produce sexual arousal, but which exploits and dehumanizes sex so that human beings are treated as things and women, in particular, as sex objects.'

By the time the Williams Committee presented its report there had been a change of Government, so that the Home Secretary who received it on 31st October (Halloween!) 1979 was William Whitelaw.

Mary Whitehouse, who had submitted recommendations to the committee on behalf of the National Viewers and Listeners Association, had been promised an advanced copy, to be collected from the Home Office at 2.00 p.m. She had invited Charles to meet her in the foyer there so that together they could try to digest the 269-page report as quickly as possible. Fortunately there was a seven-page summary! Within minutes they were whisked away by taxi to BBC and ITV studios for radio and television interviews for the early evening news bulletins.

The two campaigners for public morality were dismayed by the report of the Williams Committee. 'In a word,' said Charles, 'the recommendations of the report were permissive. It suggested that pornographic material of any degree of obscenity should be available for all persons of 18 years and over, provided it was sold in shops which did not display pornography in the window and under 18's were not allowed inside.'

Although the Home Secretary put the report 'on the shelf', Soho pornographers were quick to respond. Within a week, pornographic shops with blackened windows were selling the most appalling obscene magazines, videos, films and sexual paraphernalia. Across one window were emblazoned the words 'As recommended by the Williams Report'.

The floodgates duly opened. 'Sex shops', as they came to be called, began to appear in towns and cities across the country. Within weeks there were eighty-four such establishments in a square quarter of a mile in Soho. David Sullivan, who had a criminal record for 'living off immoral earnings' and had made a fortune out of pornographic films, set up a company to buy lock-up shops, in order to rent them out to another company, Conegate Ltd (later changed to Quietlynn Ltd) to sell adult magazines. Planning permission was not required for change of use of the premises. In towns where these shops opened, local people raised their protest, but there was no legal basis for demanding closure and there was much confusion and frustration.

In 1981, in the St Helens newspaper, Charles spotted an advertisement for a manager of an adult bookshop soon to be opened in the town. He made enquiries at the town's thirteen estate agents to try and find the site but drew a blank at all of them. He therefore gave himself a pseudonym and sent off an application for the job, asking when and where the shop was to open. By return he was offered the job without interview and given the address and opening date, three weeks ahead. It was a corner shop, very near the town centre, where an old-fashioned bespoke tailor was still trading. The elderly proprietor had inherited the business from his father, but had now decided to sell up and retire.

'Do you know what kind of shop it's going to be?' asked Charles.

'Oh yes,' replied the old gentleman, 'the men from London said it would be a boutique selling suede jackets and modern gear.' He was appalled when he learned the truth. Charles offered to buy the premises from him for the same price plus all the legal costs, but the old man reluctantly declined as he did not want the least delay in the sale going through.

Charles' next move was to book St Helens Town Hall for a protest meeting, and although it was a cold wet February night, 600 people turned out to express determined opposition to the proposed sex shop. The following evening, a hundred and thirty volunteers formed an Action Group. Local newspapers responded marvellously, giving full coverage to a protest march through the town and to the silent vigil set up outside the shop while it was still a tailor's. Two-hour shifts throughout working hours brought together a Church of England vicar and a Roman Catholic priest with members of a Brethren assembly, as well as other people with objections other than Christian ones to the opening of a sex shop in their town.

Charles sent newspaper cuttings about the St Helens protest to Brian Richards, managing director of Conegate, telling him that the people of the town would not stand by and let him open a sex shop there. He also offered to buy the premises from the company for the

£15,500 agreed with the tailor plus legal costs. By then, however, repair work had been carried out and with some alterations and rewiring, the total price Conegate wanted would now be £19,000. After two weeks of negotiations a deal was agreed for the premises to be bought from Conegate and sold to a thriving paint and wallpaper business which occupied the adjoining premises. One clause in the contract ensured that Conegate would not open a sex shop anywhere within a five-mile radius of St Helens town centre. As a director of the company commented to a *Daily Star* reporter, 'We don't go where we're not wanted. I can only say they must be an extremely Christian lot in St Helens.' That view was confirmed by an attendance of four hundred people at a thanksgiving service for the successful outcome of the protest.

When rumours began to circulate about the opening of a sex shop in the Wavertree district of Liverpool, local residents—mostly mothers—organised a public meeting in a school hall. Anthony Steen, MP for Wavertree, also held a meeting with city councillors and other interested parties; afterwards a Wavertree Action Group was set up. Charles Oxley was asked to be its chairman and a plan of campaign was drawn up. A parliamentary petition was begun and eleven thousand signatures were very quickly obtained. It was presented at the House of Commons but achieved little, as there was no legislation which could prevent the opening of such a shop.

The Action Group organised a rota, consisting mainly of mothers and church leaders, who stood outside the shop in a silent vigil from 8.00 a.m. to 6.00 p.m. in all weathers, throughout nine months that included a very cold winter. Conversations took place during these hours which encouraged the faith of many of the ladies taking part. There was a healthy mixture from various denominations and other people with no church commitment. About halfway through the campaign Charles asked a Roman Catholic priest if he would take over as chairman and he agreed to do so.

Charles had by now received a number of requests from towns wanting help in their fight against sex shops; among them were Wigan, Preston, Southport, Sefton and Hartlepool. He spoke at many council meetings, giving what information he could on the companies who were applying for a licence to operate the shops.

Christian MPs were trying to introduce legislation which would make it impossible, or at least very difficult, to obtain licences, and eventually a clause was passed giving the authority to local councils to grant or refuse licences under the Local Government (Miscellaneous Provisions) Bill. Most councils were very willing to use this legislation to refuse applications, but the legal procedure for appeal was so complicated that the company could continue to apply for a licence on appeal, even though one had been refused. Conegate became expert at this device and would continue to operate the shop and drag out the procedure for many months after a licence had been refused.

Working with Mary Whitehouse, Charles sent out leaflets giving advice to people involved in these legal battles. Each leaflet ran to three pages of A4 paper and went into very precise detail about how to approach the local authority; the kind of letter to write to the appropriate officer; it also suggested paying a visit to the actual shop so as to report to the police any material considered indecent; it urged protesters to be sure to attend any hearing and gave this advice: 'The hearing is not a law court and there is no cause for any objector to feel nervous or embarrassed. Do not allow yourself to be intimidated or bamboozled.'

The success of a battle campaign often depends on how well you know your enemy's strategy, so Charles' leaflet warned about the content of a one-and-a-half-hour speech which the company's solicitor would make to the council sub-committee hearing the appeal.

Where the local protest groups were vigilant and determined, success usually followed. In Southport, where as many as 1500 people attended a protest meeting and 18,000 signed a petition, the campaign lasted three years and eight

A regular visitor to the House of Commons, here in 1982 presenting a petition opposing a sex shop in Southport with Trevor Condy, a local architect; Mary Maddock, a primary school head; Geoffrey Ellis, proprietor of Southport Christian Book Centre; and Sir Ian Percival, the town's Member of Parliament.

months from the time when the sex shop first opened until it finally closed its doors. In Hartlepool, the local newspaper's banner headline—'Anti-Porn Man to Visit Town'—heralded Charles' visit: 'Whitehouse Aide for Sex Shops Debate.' As it turned out, the local council's Development Control Sub-committee voted unanimously to reject the application for a licence without the need for Charles or other objectors to speak.

In October 1982 the BBC put Merseyside in the spotlight by broadcasting several of its major radio programmes from the area. David Jacobs hosted a recording of *Any Questions* from Bootle Town Hall, the Archers presented their everyday story of country folk from Crosby Civic Hall, and from the same venue came a *Woman's Hour* debate on the legalisation of sex shops. Producer Diana Stenson and presenter Sue MacGregor wanted to move away from the cosy fireside image of the programme, and by bringing together Charles Oxley of the Merseyside Community Standards Association and Brian Richards, managing director of the Conegate sex shop chain, they were certainly doing just that. The report in the *Liverpool Echo* carried the headline, 'Earful for sex shop radio man' and described how Mr Richards faced a verbal attack not just from Charles Oxley and Merseyside police committee chairman Mrs Margaret Simey, but also from angry housewives among the capacity four hundred audience in the Civic Hall. Diana Stenson's letter of thanks to Charles afterwards described it as 'our most successful *Woman's Hour* outside broadcast ever.'

There were several reasons why Charles found the legalisation of pornography abhorrent. 'First of all,' he said, 'pornography debases love. It claims to release people from inhibitions but in fact enslaves them to sexual desires. It leaves out commitment, responsibility, trust and love. It also exploits women by portraying them as objects for use by men rather than as real people. The young and the sexually disturbed want to imitate what they see portrayed, and that can lead to promiscuity.'

But if pornography were limited to the confines of a sex shop, would that not protect children from being affected by it?

'Not at all. The sex shop in Wavertree had children as young as 14 going in. And even if you could prevent anyone under 18 from going in, you cannot stop people from passing on a pornographic magazine after they have bought it. That's when the young are vulnerable. Another harmful effect is that the incidence of rape and attempted rape shows a clear increase of 200-300 per cent after a period in which pornography has had a freer circulation. This was mentioned by Dr Court of Australia whose submission to the Williams Committee was ignored.'

Charles' understanding of biblical principles left him in no doubt that the only legitimate sexual relationship was that between husband and wife within marriage. He referred to pre-marital sex by its traditional name of fornication, and extra-marital sex as adultery. Both were clearly wrong in the teaching of the Bible, no matter how many people might think otherwise.

Likewise, Charles' Christian beliefs led him to speak out strongly against blasphemy, which he regarded as an explicit insult directed at God or an implicit declaration of atheism. He saw it as significant that the third of the Ten Commandments, dealing with blasphemy, warns that '... the Lord will not hold him guiltless who takes His name in vain.' In Old Testament times the penalty for blasphemy was death, and in the book of Leviticus an actual instance is recorded of a man being put to death for blasphemy.

In the New Testament also Charles recognised the supreme authority and respect accorded to the name of Jesus Christ. It was in that name that the disciples were sent out to make disciples of all nations, to baptise new converts, to cast out demons, to heal the sick and raise the dead. The apostle Paul wrote of a day when '...at the name of Jesus every knee should bow, both in heaven and earth...' For anyone, then, to use the name of Jesus as a term of abuse, to express anger, frustration, contempt or hatred, would arouse the wrath of Charles Oxley. It made no difference that the blasphemer might claim not to believe in God or in Jesus Christ as the Son of God.

He was saddened by the easy acceptance of blasphemy in 'normal' conversation, particularly when that was encouraged by its frequent use on radio and television. He was stirred by the memory of his sister as a 17-year-old junior office girl in a Glasgow bank: hearing her manager take the name of the Lord in vain she said to him, 'Excuse me, but Jesus Christ is my Saviour and friend, so would you please not use his name in that way.' The manager immediately apologised and curbed his tongue from then on, at least within her hearing.

Charles found it particularly distressing to hear small children taking God's name in vain. A six-year-old in one of his schools came out with a particularly foul blasphemy when his pencil rolled off the desk to the floor, breaking the lead. His horrified teacher asked, 'Where on earth did you hear that, Simon?' The lad replied unhesitatingly, 'That's what my daddy says when the car won't start.'

In 1977 Denis Lemon published James Kirkup's poem 'The love that dares to speak its name' in *Gay News*, a magazine for homosexuals. Alongside a nude figure of Christ on the cross, and with vulgar expression and cheap jibes, it told of homosexual activity by Jesus with his disciples and others. In fetid language it described loathsome sexual assaults on the body of Christ when taken down from the cross. The author took up the centurion's confession of faith in Jesus as the Son of God and shamelessly tried to twist it into a justification for sodomy.

Lemon and his associates were banking on the fact that laws against blasphemy had been taken off the statute book in 1967 and 1969, but they had overlooked the Common Law of blasphemous libel. It was this which Mary Whitehouse took up to bring a private prosecution against Lemon and the magazine.

In seeking support for Mrs Whitehouse's stand on this important issue, Charles made a round trip of 200 miles to speak to an eminent clergyman. On arrival, though an appointment had been made, he was told, 'His Grace is unable to see you.' Charles left the relevant papers with the secretary, requesting an early response. No response came. A telephone enquiry ten days later elicited the information that His Grace had put the papers on the fire. After the case had been successfully concluded, with the editor and magazine heftily fined, and the publicity over, His Grace sent a smarmy handwritten letter of congratulation to 'Dear Mary...' Charles' reaction? 'Ugh! Ashes on his mitre!'

His Grace was not alone, as churchmen of various denominations poured scorn on Mrs Whitehouse's prosecution and the very idea of bringing such a case to court. A Norwich clergyman wrote to *The Times* (23rd July 1977): 'If (the Christ who emerges from the case) is to be regarded as a twentieth-century Saviour, He will need to toughen up... Christians would do better to study these matters rather than dash off to defend Jesus in the Old Bailey by invoking laws which have lain dormant for fifty years.'

During the autumn of 1977 and the spring of 1978 many letters on the subject were published in the correspondence columns of Christian Weekly Newspaper publications and *The Church Times*. In Charles' estimation they served to show how muddled was the thinking of so many churchmen, both Anglican and others, on the issue of blasphemy. He could not resist entering the fray.

One correspondent had written that he could justify the silence of church leaders on the grounds that they were following the example of Jesus in remaining silent when accused before the chief priests. Replied Charles: 'There are several significant differences. Jesus had already condemned the chief priests in very strong terms; he was surrounded by false witnesses and the court had already decided to put him to death; he was condemned for telling the truth. *Gay News* was condemned for telling lies and telling them in a particularly obnoxious manner.'

Barbara Smoker, president of the National Secular Society, had written to *The Church Times* complaining about Mary Whitehouse's action in bringing the prosecution in the first place, claiming that we were 'an adult society not needing a school marm.' Her letter drew this response from Charles:—

> I would describe a society as 'adult', when it is discerning in what is right and wrong, self-disciplined, considerate for the feelings of others and responsible in its caring for its young and immature members. Miss Smoker uses the word 'adult' as do those who advertise 'X' certificate films and pornographic paperbacks meaning more permissive and explicit in the portrayal of sex and violence.
>
> If Mrs Whitehouse had acted as a school marm, she would not have instituted legal proceedings against Denis Lemon. She would have smacked his bottom.
>
> But the law against blasphemy was not invented by Mrs Whitehouse. It is God's law, and Miss Smoker's quarrel is with Him.

It was on 12th July 1977 when an Old Bailey jury brought in a Guilty verdict on Denis Lemon and *Gay News* on a charge of blasphemous libel. On 7th August 1977 a committee was formed to campaign for the abolition of the law against blasphemy. The offending poem was re-published in the *Anarchist Worker, Socialist Challenge, Peace News, Liberator* and *Freedom*; and copies of the poem were handed to members of the public.

At the time of the appeal in February 1978, the National Gay News Defence Committee organised a march and rally in Trafalgar Square, expressing support for *Gay News* and opposition to the law against blasphemy.

Denis Lemon lost his appeal and, as Guest of Honour the following evening at the annual dinner of the National Secular Society, he asked, 'Should we now expect prosecution for all those who have re-published the poem?'

Nicolas Walter, editor of *New Humanist*, in a speech in Brighton three weeks before the appeal, said, 'Mrs Whitehouse must be shown that she cannot stop the poem being read. But freedom does not come from the public meetings and lobbying MPs. It has to be taken, not asked for. This should be done by circulating the poem.'

William McIlroy was formerly editor of *Freethinker*, the journal of the National Secular Society, which had campaigned for the abolition of laws against blasphemy and obscenity, the abolition of laws restricting Sunday trade and sport, the abolition of Religious Education in schools, the lowering of the age of consent, the raising of the age of criminal responsibility, the total acceptance of homosexual practices, easier divorce, abortion on demand and euthanasia. As honorary secretary of the Committee Against Blasphemy Law, William McIlroy solicited support for a statement deploring the *Gay News* trial and verdict, and calling for a repeal of all legal sanctions against blasphemy.

The Committee tried to give the impression that intellectuals and perceptive Christians were opposed to a law against blasphemy. In January 1978, McIlroy published a list of some 140 supporters, including 12 peers, 10 MPs, 9 professors, 4 churchmen, some writers and journalists and a concert pianist. Charles Oxley felt it would have been quite wrong for the impression to be given that all intellectuals and perceptive Christians opposed the blasphemy law, so he sought to match McIlroy's list by writing to about 300 people whom he expected to be willing to express public support for 'the retention of present (1978) legal restraint on blasphemy.' One hundred and eighty persons did so, including 13 peers, 9 MPs, 14 professors, 38 churchmen, several writers, broadcasters, actors and head teachers.

A strong supporter of the National Secular Society, Lord Ted Willis, the former television script writer, tried hard to have blasphemy removed from common law. In a House of Lords debate on 23rd February 1978 his Bill failed to get a second reading, but not before a succession of noble lords, both temporal and spiritual, had argued elegantly and forcefully for over three and a half hours. It was that kind of occasion, when the upper chamber shows a depth of feeling—and logic—which down the centuries made it a very special place. Lord Willis himself quoted Scripture several times in his eloquent speech, and he threw this direct challenge at the 'leaders of the Established Church', some of whom were present to hear him: 'Why does the Church stand aside and leave the dirty work to a small extremist fringe group? Why hide behind the skirts of Mrs Mary Whitehouse?' He described the blasphemy law as 'an unsavoury relic of history, conceived in fear, rooted in religious privilege, stained with prejudice and an ever-present threat to the greatest morality of all, the morality of liberty of thought.'

The Earl of Halsbury led the opposition to the Bill: 'I think that society has suffered enough damage in recent years at the hands of the so-called liberal humanists. They plunder the capital accumulated by 2,000 years of Christian effort and thereby provide the backcloth of an ostensible respectability. Against this, they preach that Christian values are unnecessary, that we can get along without them, though, of course, they are living, albeit without very much insight, on Christian values at second-hand. They then embark upon the destruction of those values for no better reason than to give themselves something to write about.'

In his closing words, the Earl summed up the feelings of probably a very large silent majority, and definitely those of a very vocal campaigner, Charles Oxley, when he said, 'I have had enough of not the "permissive" but the "licentious" society in which I have lived for the past thirty years and I want to strike a blow in the defence of something better.'

In May 1981 the Law Commission published a working party's report on blasphemy law, so Charles took the opportunity to express his views to the Commission. He wanted the blasphemy law not only retained but strengthened and widened: 'strengthened so that it covers not only blasphemous libel but also any misuse of the name of God and Jesus Christ in print or in broadcasting; widened to extend to other main religions.'

In his local area, through the St Helens Christian Council, he pressed for ordinary people to be able to have their say on blasphemy, and the Christian Council organised a petition to be circulated among the churches in the town.

Mary Whitehouse's prosecution of Denis Lemon and *Gay News* served not only to deal with one gross instance of blasphemous libel but also to make people think whether they were prepared to see another stone removed from the crumbling edifice of Christian morality. It was not that God or Jesus Christ needed the law to protect them. In the words of Lord Scarman, dismissing the *Gay News* appeal to the House of Lords in 1979: 'The offence belongs to a group of criminal offences designed to safeguard the internal tranquillity of the nation ... I will not lend my voice to a view of the law of blasphemous libel which would render it a dead letter or diminish its efficacy to protect religious feeling from outrage and insult.'

Chapter 7

PUNISH THE WICKED, CARE FOR THE VICTIMS

First prize for the daftest remark in years must surely go to the social worker who appeared in a Metropolitan Magistrates' Court on behalf of a 15-year-old boy. The boy had committed fifty-two crimes, including burglary, theft and malicious wounding. He had broken into a pet shop and killed all the animals, and he had set fire to a railway station.

In reply to the magistrate's comment on this appalling record, the social worker said, 'This lad would not have such a bad record if the police would not keep arresting him.'

Such a remark highlighted for Charles Oxley and many others the way in which official attitudes to law and order changed in perhaps two generations. Right up to the 1950s a policeman who caught a boy up to mischief in the street would give him a clip round the ear and take the lad home to his parents, who would probably give him their own swift and painful punishment. Today, the policeman would be charged with assault and the boy would be assigned a social worker.

The Conservative Party has traditionally seen itself as the party of law and order, so when the Tories came to power in 1979 and a debate on the return of capital punishment followed in July of that year, Charles took the opportunity to write to William Whitelaw, the new Home Secretary. He wrote as Chairman of the Campaign for Law and Order, whose official address—ironically—was Princes Road, Toxteth, Liverpool 8, the focal point two years later of rioting and disorder.

The letter dealt with the arguments advanced for the abolition of capital punishment before listing positive reasons why it should be reintroduced. One argument put forward by the abolitionists is that the deterrent effect of the death penalty cannot be proved. Charles regarded this as an upside-down argument:—

The onus is on the politicians to prove that the number of unlawful killings has decreased as a result of abolition in 1965. This they cannot do. One cannot calculate how many more people will kill when the penalty is a few years in prison, but would not kill if it incurs the death penalty. Yet common sense tells us that the death penalty is feared more than prison.

But argument about deterrence is based on *expediency*, whereas the question is really a matter of *principle*. Is it right or wrong? That brings the question back to one of authority.

For Charles, that meant the authority of God as revealed in the Bible; a just God required retribution for crime and the only adequate retribution for deliberate murder is death.

In answer to those who claim that hanging is degrading in a civilised society, Charles asserted that murder and violence are also degrading, and with the amount of violent crime these days we have forfeited the right to describe ourselves as civilised. He was not in favour of hanging as the method of execution, although inevitably the headline-writers refer to a call for the return of the death penalty as a call for hanging.

Since the release of those such as the wrongly convicted 'Guildford Four', the argument has been strong that it is unsafe to have capital punishment in case an innocent person is executed. Charles was definitely on thin ice here, asserting that this possibility is very tiny. He was more concerned that released murderers, having had a 'life' sentence of perhaps ten years, were then free to murder again. There were thirty-seven instances of that happening between 1973 and 1983.

But would not juries hesitate to bring in a Guilty verdict if they knew that the death sentence would follow? 'That,' said Charles, 'is a slanderous accusation. Juries can and must be trusted to bring in a true verdict based on the evidence alone. It is for the trial judge, the appeal court and the Home Secretary to exercise the prerogative of mercy when it is justified.'

To the claim that terrorists would become martyrs and that hostages might be taken to try and secure the release of captured terrorists, Charles replied that this was a defeatist argument. 'It is an admission that terrorism is out of hand and that justice is in retreat.'

As well as attempting to answer the arguments of the abolitionists, Charles put forward his own beliefs. Basing his viewpoint on Romans chapter 13 and verses 1-4, he claimed that the State has not only the *right* but actually also the *duty* to punish evildoers, including among its sanctions the taking of life, in order to protect its people: '...The authorities that exist have been established by God... Rulers hold no terror for those who do right, but for those who do wrong. Do you want to be free from fear of the one in authority? Then do what is right... But if you do wrong, be afraid, for he does not bear the sword for nothing. He is God's servant, an agent of wrath to bring punishment on the wrongdoer.' (New International Version) The Authorised Version has this final sentence in these words: '... for he is the minister of God, a revenger to execute wrath upon him that doeth evil.' Charles was convinced that because the civil authorities did not fulfil their duty to impose adequate punishments on wrongdoers, respect for those authorities had seriously deteriorated so that lawlessness was now rife.

He felt that the matter was not one for politicians to decide. 'It is a moral question which affects the whole nation and the whole nation should decide in a referendum.' He thought that MPs were supremely arrogant in ignoring the known demands of the large majority of their constituents, thus bringing the House of Commons into disrepute. Those who voted against capital punishment were in effect saying that the life of a murderer is of more value than the life of his victim. It was the close relatives of murder victims whose views Charles wanted to be heeded most, also the opinions of ordinary policemen and prison officers who had to deal with murderers.

In his letter to the Home Secretary in July 1979, Charles repeated the question he had put to successive Home Secretaries without ever receiving the courtesy of a reply: 'At what point will you admit that present policies have failed?' The appalling rise in violent crime coincided with the abolition of capital and corporal punishment; nobody doubted the sincerity of those who took the decisions to abolish these sanctions, but events have proved them to be mistaken.

Such deep convictions as these lay at the heart of the Campaign for Law and Order. In its list of aims and objectives, published in a pamphlet in May 1976, the CLO stated: 'The aim of the Campaign is to work by lawful means for the restoration of law and order by effective punishment, including capital and corporal punishment for certain degrees of crime. Membership is open to all persons regardless of political belief, race or creed.'

The CLO was quite prepared to specify crimes for which capital punishment should be reintroduced:—

> Acts of terrorism resulting in death. Premeditated murder. Deliberate murder. Sexual assault resulting in death. Murder in the furtherance of theft. Murder of a member of a police force or the prison service whilst in execution of his/her duty.

Similarly, the Campaign demanded corporal punishment for the following:—

> Wanton attack on the person. Rape and sexual assault. Robbery or attempted robbery with violence. Persistent physical cruelty to wife and/or children. Violence resulting in serious injury to a child or adult person. Assault on a member of a police force or the prison service whilst in execution of his/her duty. Acts of vandalism and especially terrorism of elderly persons. Wanton cruelty to animals.

As Chairman of the Campaign for Law and Order, Charles produced a twice-yearly Bulletin which was circulated to all paid-up members. His own filing system came in very handy for this job, as he made a habit of taking newspaper cuttings on a variety of subjects. His study contained dozens of ring binders and foolscap folders carefully documenting the nation's decline into spiritual and moral decay, so that when a Bulletin was due, he could extract relevant stories, letters, comments from public figures, crime statistics, and add his own personal comments.

In the last Bulletin that Charles produced, in January 1987, he wrote of 'Headaches and Heartaches': the former were the unavailing attempts to persuade the Home Office that law and order were in serious decline and needed a swift change in methods of punishment; the latter were the individuals who had suffered at the hands of muggers, rapists, kidnappers and murderers. The Bulletin warmly commended Geoffrey Dickens MP, a strong supporter of the CLO, in his attempts to strengthen the law on the murder of a child. Likewise, the Bulletin offered 'heartiest congratulations to James Anderton, Chief Constable of Greater Manchester, for his strong denunciation of sexual perversions and permissiveness. Predictably, it raised squeals of protest from his Police Authority, but he courageously claimed he spoke with a higher authority. He received thousands of letters of support. All this is in sharp contrast to the timid pronouncements of the Archbishops of Canterbury and York, who spoke of homosexuality as a handicap and a misfortune without condemning sodomy as sin.'

A concluding 'Message from the Chairman' urged members to canvass their friends, relatives and work colleagues to support the CLO so that the all-too-silent majority could be heard. The final line of the Bulletin then showed that the CLO Chairman had his own problems with the criminal fraternity from time to time: 'I arrested two burglars on our premises recently and will write about it in the next Bulletin.'

The incident to which Charles referred was far from being isolated, Tower College being anything but an ivory tower! Set in its own grounds behind a high wall, and with open ground at the back sweeping down for nearly a mile to the M62 motorway, it was a favourite target for intruders. Sometimes it was no more than a few local lads intent on some vandalism or minor theft and Charles would readily give chase on foot or in his car around the neighbourhood. There were also, though, the more professional and sinister intruders; Charles knew that if he had an overnight stop in Scotland or London, it left his home (and his wife and daughter) vulnerable.

On one occasion, Charles and his youngest son, Danny, were both at home with Muriel and Rachel when a burglar made too much noise in his search for valuables. Although it was well after midnight,

Charles was still at work in his study on the first floor when he heard the tell-tale sounds. Creeping along the corridor, he cornered the intruder in a bathroom, whereupon the man hit out at Charles, who replied with a punch to the head. Sounds of a struggle brought Danny to the scene, so that the burglar now had to contend with two six-foot-four, sixteen-stone Oxleys. It was no contest, of course, and when the police arrived to apprehend the man, he claimed to have been subjected to a violent and unprovoked attack by Oxley senior. Charles told him off as if he had been a second-form pupil and the man was led away.

Charles' black-and-white view of so many law and order matters brought him into conflict with those who felt that there were also some 'grey' areas or that his ideas were too extreme. The correspondence columns of Merseyside newspapers provided the battlefield more than once between Charles Oxley and Liverpool's Deputy Chief Probation Officer, David Mathieson. Mr Mathieson, a Methodist local preacher, saw no value in harsh treatment for offenders or in long prison sentences; he advocated rehabilitation as a major strand in the treatment of even the most serious offenders. Charles would have none of it, asserting that it was the retreat from firm punishment which had allowed the crime figures to soar. He complained when the Home Secretary recommended shorter prison sentences, but Mr Mathieson agreed with the proposal, accusing Charles of being 'confused and illogical', 'totally inaccurate' and 'deliberately misleading'. Charles was sure his views coincided with those of a large majority of ordinary people. 'And as long as soft-headed sociologists and crackpot criminologists have their way, the crime rate will continue to rise,' he wrote to the *Liverpool Daily Post* in 1980.

When the numbers of those out of work reached more than three million, some were claiming that unemployment was a cause of crime. In 1982 the unemployment rate for Merseyside was 20% and in the first seven months of that year crime in the region had risen by 10.5%. The Liberal MP for Liverpool Mossley Hill was David (now Lord) Alton. Both he and Shirley Williams, who was the Social Democratic Party MP for Crosby at that time, attacked Mrs Thatcher's policies for undermining the social fabric of the country and thereby contributing to the increase in crime. Charles Oxley's letter to the

Liverpool Daily Post on 2nd August 1982 suggested that Mr Alton and Mrs Williams had the wrong end of the stick and that it was crime which caused unemployment rather than the other way round.

> Many businesses which would have employed local people have moved out of inner-city areas because of crime and vandalism mostly undetected, hardly ever punished and virtually uncontrollable.
>
> From personal experience over seven years in Toxteth, I can tell you that business people can expect to have their windows broken, the lead stripped from their roof, rubbish dumped over their walls, their premises repeatedly broken into, their vehicles stolen by 'joy-riding' youths who are likely to smash them up and their employees mugged on their way to and from work.
>
> When law and order are restored to Toxteth, then boarded-up shops and shut-down factories will re-open and create employment.
>
> (See Chapter 8 for Charles' personal experiences in the Toxteth riots.)

The proposal to reintroduce either capital or corporal punishment always rouses strong feelings on both sides. The Campaign for Law and Order organised a lobby of Parliament, and Charles arranged for a special train to take 150 supporters from the north-west of England down to London; they included 70 people who themselves had been the victims of violent attacks.

In all, there were four hundred people in the Grand Committee Room of the Palace of Westminster, with Charles chairing the meeting. Robert Kilroy-Silk, in his pre-television days, was the MP for Ormskirk at that time, and his constituency included what was a fairly notorious town—Kirkby—before boundary changes separated the towns. He and other MPs spoke of their opposition to the reintroduction of corporal punishment for crimes of violence and capital punishment for premeditated murder and terrorism. The response from some of Kilroy-Silk's constituents was blunt and forthright: they told him they were afraid to go out even in the daytime for fear of being attacked and they were constantly being terrorised by vandals around the blocks of flats which abounded in the area. They told him that he should represent the views of his constituents rather than follow his party's line.

Among those who supported the CLO's demands were other north-west MPs—Graham Page (Crosby), Ian Percival (Southport) and Cyril Smith (Rochdale).

Further pressure from the CLO came in the form of a petition in 1982, signed by over half a million people asking Parliament for a national referendum on the reintroduction of capital punishment. Charles was one of the group that presented the petition at the House of Commons on a day when MPs were debating the Criminal Justice Bill. However, on that occasion, as on every other one since, those against capital punishment won the day.

What incensed Charles was seeing piles of petition forms being thrown into paper sacks marked 'FOR BURNING'. So much for the will of the people in a parliamentary democracy where polls show up to 80% of the population in favour of the return of capital punishment for certain categories of murder!

Charles recognised that his opponents were strong and numerous. In one of his letters to the local press he listed supporters of what he called the 'Let's Be Kind To Criminals' Campaign; they included the Howard League for Penal Reform, the National Council for Civil Liberties and more than a dozen Merseyside MPs from both Labour and Conservative parties. Beyond them all, however, he knew that it was the Home Secretary who had to be persuaded to change his views, and successive holders of that post refused to budge. Even when a judge recommended that life imprisonment for a convicted murderer should extend for the rest of his life, the Home Secretary could overrule that judgement at a later date.

That is exactly what happened in the case of John G Robinson, who in 1962 was sentenced to life imprisonment. The judge told him, 'You will go to prison for the rest of your life,' yet in 1976 Robinson was released and in October of that year committed another horrible murder. Charles wrote to the Home Secretary asking why Robinson had been released after what the judge had said and was given what he regarded as a preposterous reply: 'Anything they (judges) said in open court was not of any special force and words such as "Go to prison for the rest of your life" were often used loosely.'

Sometimes it was the judges themselves who were too lenient. In 1985 a thirty-one-year-old man was released on probation after pleading guilty to four indecent assaults in one day, two of them on thirteen-year-old girls. He had drawn a knife in order to frighten the girls into removing their underclothing before the assaults took place. The judge remarked: 'These were absolutely dreadful offences, including a very nasty, vicious and dreadful attack on two young girls. But it is clear to me that you had, in simple terms, a complete breakdown. I am going to take an exceptional course and not send you to prison.'

Members of Parliament were not slow to voice their loud disapproval of the judge's action. Charles Oxley went further. The *Liverpool Daily Post* headline on 31st August 1985 proclaimed: 'Oxley Blasts "Lenient" Judges', and he was quoted as saying, 'Judges who let off child sex attackers should be sacked and locked up themselves because they are a disgrace to their profession and a danger to society.'

Similarly, he expressed public outrage at a murder conviction being changed to manslaughter when a father had smothered his seventeen-day-old son. The appeal court ruled that the father was 'provoked', because the baby had cried for five hours. A life sentence was reduced to five years. The *Today* newspaper asked for Charles' comments. 'Babies have cried since the world began,' he said.

In 1985 Charles read of a new organisation campaigning for law and order, called the 'Law and Order Society'. He approached the leaders immediately, arranged a meeting and it was agreed that they should work together. From this came the realisation that there were other groups too, each with its own particular emphasis but with the same general objectives, so Charles suggested calling together the leaders of these groups to explore the possibility of forming a federation. In all, eleven organisations were represented at a meeting in the Central Hall, Westminster, at which it was agreed to establish an organisation to be called the 'Nation Federation of Campaigners for Law and Order'. Each member group would retain its own identity and have complete autonomy. Charles Oxley was elected Chairman of the new NFCLO.

The advantages of forming this federation were that people with specialised knowledge, varied experience, a wider range of useful contacts and membership support from almost every parliamentary constituency in the country, could together mount increased pressure on those responsible for law and order. A second meeting enabled members to agree on the following main demands:

1 A reversal of the 'be kind to criminals' policy with much greater concern for the victims of crime.
2 An even-handed enforcement of the rule of law in policing, in prosecuting and in sentencing.
3 The restoration of police control over its own operations with adequate manpower and free from political interference.
4 The immediate introduction of the death penalty for wilful murder.
5 The availability of corporal punishment for those convicted of grievous bodily harm, sexual assault or cruelty, especially against a child or elderly person.
6 The maintenance of English Common Law and opposition to its erosion, particularly where this undermines law and order.
7 Full support for the Royal Ulster Constabulary in its heroic fight against terrorism.
8 Full support for the establishment of neighbourhood watch schemes to help police in the fight against crime.

At the Conservative Party Conference in Blackpool in 1985, the Campaign for Law and Order arranged a fringe meeting in one of the seafront hotels in the town. Both Charles, as Chairman, and Geoffrey Dickens MP, as guest speaker, were widely reported in the news media in their criticism of the apparent 'softly, softly' approach to criminals and in their call for Parliament to pass legislation to protect children from sexual abuse. Among those taking part in an open forum were Mrs Ann West, mother of Moors murder victim Lesley Ann Downey, and Mrs Dianne Core of Child Watch. When the proprietor of the Fernley Hotel, where the meeting was held, found out its purpose, he refused to charge the CLO for the use of his facilities.

Charles saw clearly that a contributory factor in the deterioration of law and order was the erosion of traditional family life. In an article entitled *Suffer Little Children* he presented a chilling catalogue of cases in which children had been brutally murdered by their parents or 'live-in lovers'. Public inquiries into some of these cases had shown the social services in a bad light, because battered children had been returned to their natural parents. 'But the failures of social workers and others must not be allowed to obscure the fact that the blame lies primarily with the parents.'

Charles' daughter Rachel worked for two years in a residential home for children under seven in local authority care. She was horrified at the appalling cruelty inflicted by parents on babies and small children. She told her father that some mothers were totally incapable of caring for babies and toddlers, losing their temper at the slightest thing and venting their anger with verbal and physical abuse on the unfortunate child. Even worse, she told him, there were parents who woke their children up in the middle of the night so as to inflict pain and torture on them. It was particularly distressing for Rachel to see children, nursed back to health and happiness with loving care, then returning to their parents, since the nurses knew full well that in a matter of days, even hours, the children would be back in hospital with cigarette burns, bruises, black eyes or broken bones.

Charles felt that there should be no stigma attached to parents who admitted that they could not cope with their children and allowed their offspring to go to live with foster parents or be adopted. The wise King Solomon had recognised that it was the woman who loved her child who had been prepared to give it up.

'Battered babies are the victims of the permissive society,' asserted Charles, 'which has now become the vicious and violent society. The Divorce Reform Act (1969) undermined the sanctity of marriage and the stability of home life, causing untold misery to hundreds of young children whose lives have been torn apart emotionally. As the Christian view of marriage is abandoned and as adultery becomes increasingly acceptable, we can expect many more child murders.'

Charles had no doubt either about the role which television and radio played in the erosion of family life.

> Night after night, our TV screens portray fornication and adultery as normal and acceptable behaviour. Domestic tension seems to be the essential theme for radio plays. Verbal and physical violence is now the indispensable element in TV entertainment. Complaints and protests to the BBC and IBA receive a polite brush-off with the standard excuse of the need for realism and authenticity and they are very sorry if you have been offended.

Society's complacent acceptance of a lack of respect for marriage vows was seen as an increasing problem.

> It is common practice in today's permissive society for a husband and father to desert his wife and go off with another woman. The deserted wife, with perhaps a toddler and a baby, allows a 'boyfriend' to move in. He resents the natural and legitimate demands of the small children on their mother, and, assuming the role of the father, with the right to chastise, expresses his frustration and anger by beating the unfortunate children, often brutally, sometimes fatally. *The 'live-in lover' is potentially lethal.*

Firm punishment would not by itself ensure the safety of children from vicious attacks by those who should be caring for them.

> We must re-establish Christian standards of morality, which sees marriage as Holy Matrimony, children as a gift of God and parental loving care as a reflection of the love of God.

One idea which Charles had in the 1970s has gained wide acceptance in recent years. Hearing of a nine-year-old boy threatening to stab a St Helens woman as she travelled home from a shopping expedition to Liverpool, Charles told the *St Helens Reporter* that such incidents were not uncommon and he believed it right that parents should be punished for the crimes of their offspring who were under the age of criminal responsibility. 'If a child under the age of criminal responsibility attacked someone with a knife, then we'd propose that the parent faced the assault charges. It may sound harsh but we are sure that this would give parents a real incentive to concern themselves with their children's upbringing.'

All too often, however, it was the parents who were setting the wrong example to their children. Addressing the annual conference of the Independent Schools Association in Chester in 1982, Charles said it was unreasonable to expect a higher standard of work and conduct from pupils than was expected from society generally. 'We reprimand our pupils for swearing but they hear adults swear and blaspheme quite freely. We punish pupils who steal, but many of them know that their parents "knock things off" from their place of work and justify it as a kind of economic readjustment.' He told the delegates from over 300 schools that youngsters were lectured when found with pornographic magazines, 'yet it is a multi-million-pound industry allowed to flourish with only token resistance from the Home Office.'

In April 1977 the National Campaign for Law and Order opened a new department called Victims of Violence. Charles and some of his CLO colleagues were appalled at the lack of help offered to people who had themselves been mugged and robbed or members of their families had suffered rape or murder. So much care and attention seemed to be lavished on the offenders while many an elderly pensioner dared not go out in the daytime and feared to stay in at night. In addition to physical injury and possibly permanent disfigurement, some victims never recovered from the shock of the attack. The theft of money caused real hardship, and the loss of such things as pension books, bus passes and treasured photographs of a deceased wife, husband, son or daughter brought deep distress.

Charles had a formidable ally in setting up this new area of CLO activity. Mrs Joan Jonker, a Liverpool housewife, combined a warm practical sympathy for the victims of violence with a fierce determination to make MPs and the general public aware of their plight. (Her story is told in *Victims of Violence* by Joan Jonker.)

By publicising this new branch of CLO, by reading of violent crimes in the newspapers and by advertising in the press for victims to contact them, Mrs Jonker and Charles quickly found themselves visiting terrified elderly people around the Liverpool area. Such people often did not even know of the existence of the Criminal Injuries Compensation Board and few of them could manage either to contact the Board or fill in a necessary form without help. The boot of Charles' car had several boxes of chocolates in it as gifts for those they visited, and soon Mrs Jonker was going regularly to attend to individuals who needed comforting and encouragement.

Within a year, 400 people on Merseyside had joined the ranks of Victims of Violence. Charles organised (and paid for) coach outings for groups of them. Their activities were featured in newspaper articles and on BBC Television's *Nationwide*. The Church TV Centre made a film—*Sentenced to Live*—mainly on Merseyside, to illustrate the long-term effects of criminal assault on the victims, and this too gained valuable publicity for the cause.

When Charles heard of special prayers to be said in churches for prisoners, he decided to hold a special service for victims of violence. It was to be no hole-in-the-corner affair, either, as he approached and gained the support of the Archdeacon of Liverpool to hold the service in the city's great Anglican cathedral. In his sermon the Archdeacon, Canon Charles Corbett, said that five violent crimes occurred every day within a mile of the cathedral and that society had become too tolerant of violence.

Eventually Victims of Violence became a separate charity with Joan Jonker as its Chairman and some eminent people among its Patrons: Lord Foot, Jane Ewart-Biggs, the Rt Rev. David Sheppard (Bishop of Liverpool), the Rt Rev. Maurice Wood (Bishop of St Albans), Rev. the Lord Soper. The BBC made a 50-minute *Man Alive* programme in October 1980 about the charity's work in bringing help to more than a thousand victims in Liverpool. The accompanying feature in *Radio Times* was entitled 'St Joan of Merseyside'.

Meanwhile, Charles pressed ahead with his work in the Campaign for Law and Order, urging changes in the law, stiffer sentences for the perpetrators of violent crime and the death sentence for murderers. 'Until there is a greater respect for God's laws in this nation,' he said, 'we will increasingly be victims of vandalism, victims of villainy and victims of violence.'

Chapter 8

RELIGIOUS EDUCATION AND RIOTS

Early in 1976, Raymond Johnston of the Nationwide Festival of Light, Lady Lothian of the Order of Christian Unity, Mary Whitehouse of the National Viewers and Listeners Association and Charles Oxley formed themselves into a committee to mount a campaign—'Save Religious Education'. A major weapon in their armoury was a petition which gained over 600,000 signatures. It kept to two straightforward statements:—

1 I support a Daily Act of Worship and Religious Education in schools.

2 I am against political philosophies such as Communism and Fascism being taught to children as alternatives to Christianity in Religious Education lessons. (As recommended in a Report recently published by the Government-backed National Foundation for Educational Research)

Charles had carefully traced the need for such a campaign to the activities of the British Humanist Association, which had tried, since its formation in 1962, to have religious education and corporate worship removed from state schools. Repeated failure led the BHA to change tactics in the 1970s, since a head-on confrontation was not going to bring about its objectives. It began to promote the idea that, through immigration, Britain had become a 'multi-faith' society in which Christianity was only one of several widely accepted religions. Religious education ought therefore to reflect this pluralism and include other world faiths such as Judaism, Hinduism, Buddhism and Islam. Moreover, because of a decline in churchgoing and in adherence to the Christian faith, room should also be made for 'non-religious life stances'. In other words, the humanists adopted the policy: 'If you can't beat them, join them.'

Fighting alongside the British Humanist Association were the National Secular Society; their president, David Tribe, made full use of the correspondence columns of the *Times Educational Supplement* to influence the thinking of teachers. 'Secularism believes that man can work out his own salvation,' he wrote; 'that whenever he has looked to the supernatural for help, the consequences have been disastrous ... Truth is reached by trial and error, by assertion and challenge.'

Among the stated aims of the NSS were 'the abolition of religious teaching and worship, and the introduction of objective, evolutionary and scientific instruction, in schools and other establishments supported by the state.' They referred to religious instruction as 'Christian indoctrination', which was 'no more defensible than the political indoctrination of children in totalitarian countries.'

The NSS also demanded the abolition of any laws interfering with the free use of Sunday for any and all recreational purposes; the reform of the marriage laws to make divorce easier; the abolition of laws on blasphemy. They published a tract on 'Swearing', commending the practice as 'a great release for bottled up indignation.' In March 1969 they printed and distributed direct to fifth and sixth form pupils 10,000 pamphlets inciting them to rebel against compulsory religious education in schools. About three hundred teachers were then reported to be sympathetic to the campaign, and contact had been made with leaders of the so-called 'pupil power' movement at that time.

Charles Oxley had carefully monitored all this, so that it came as no surprise to him when, in 1975, Geoffrey Edge, the Labour MP for Aldridge and Brownhills, declared his intention to introduce a private member's bill to remove the legal requirement of religious education in schools. Backed by the British Humanist Association, he sought to replace traditional Christian teaching with what Charles described as a Cook's tour of world religions, including also humanism, communism, even the occult. It was claimed that this was to provide more meaningful religious education in a multi-racial society, though Charles saw it as part of the wider campaign to undermine the Christian basis of so much of our cultural heritage.

At the same time the Religious Education Council set up a working party to consider the future of the Agreed Syllabus for Religious Education in schools. Two factors had a crucial influence on the report produced by that working party. One was the inclusion in its eleven-strong membership of Dr Harry Stopes-Roe, then Chairman of the British Humanist Association. His appointment raised not only eyebrows but also hackles among some Christians. When Charles was interviewed on BBC Radio Four's *Sunday* programme about the working party's report, he said, 'I don't know why the head of an anti-religious organisation should be on the Religious Education Council at all, and I don't know what the other ten members of the working party were doing because this report sets out the recommendations of the British Humanist Association and very much in their language.'

The second influencing factor was the publication of a pamphlet by the BHA entitled 'Objective, Fair and Balanced' which persuaded liberal-minded Christians to accept that changes should be made in the 1944 Education Act and the Christian faith should no longer have protection or a privileged position in religious education. Edwin Cox, the chairman of the REC working party, was interviewed on the same *Sunday* programme as Charles. He was the Senior Lecturer in Education at the University of London Institute of Education. He spoke of 'considerable change' since 1944, of 'an increase in life stances such as humanism' and of 'a religious pluralistic situation.' He wanted to see in schools 'an objective study of all life styles.'

The 'Save Religious Education' campaign mobilised its forces to counter the threat posed by the humanists and their allies. In addition to the huge petition, the four members of the committee made full use of every opportunity to put forward the arguments in favour of traditional RE, the teaching of Christianity. Mary Whitehouse wrote an article in *The Times* of June 3rd 1976 which began:

The implementation of this report would mean the virtual end of Christian religious education in schools ...

Nowhere in these proposals is there any acknowledgement that Britain is, in any sense, a Christian country with a Christian heritage. There is but one reference to the Bible, and that in a negative form. The name of Jesus Christ is mentioned not at all. No room in the inn? Still less, it would seem, in religious education ...

If ... the recommendations of this working party are accepted, this would sound the death knell in this country of the Judaeo-Christian faith which has, for more than a thousand years, been the source of our greatness, the inspiration of our great social reformers, the base of our political stability, the foundation of home and family life, the touchstone of so much of our culture.

The 'Save Religious Education' campaign did not receive wholehearted support from all branches of the Christian church. Charles wrote to the Bishop of Liverpool, the Rt Rev. David Sheppard, to ask if he would commend the campaign to the churches of his diocese. The Bishop's reply indicated that those with whom he had discussed the request had misgivings about the petition: they did not like the wording of it, they felt that the wrong questions were being addressed and that the issue was being clouded. He regretted that he was unable to commend the petition.

The wording of the petition also brought criticism from David Blair, Secretary of the Association of Christian Teachers, a group of which Charles was a very active member. On the *Sunday* programme on 1st February 1976, he described the campaign as 'hasty and ill-conceived' among other remarks which led to a lengthy correspondence between Charles and himself as each sought to clarify his own position in the eyes of the other.

Support for the campaign came from Dr Donald Coggan, the Archbishop of Canterbury, and forcefully also from Lord Hailsham. He wrote to the committee: 'The requirements of an act of worship and R I in the 1944 Act were a part of the general policy laid down in that Act and should not be made the subject of repeal or piecemeal alteration by Private Members' legislation ... You may certainly count on me to support your campaign on religious education.'

The 1944 Education Act was drawn up by R A Butler who by this time had become Lord Butler, Master of Trinity College, Cambridge.

He was equally unequivocal about the campaign: 'The provisions in the 1944 Education Act on religious teaching were warmly approved by all denominations and by the public. Based on the syllabus of religious teaching they were not intended to do more than introduce the child to the basic knowledge of the origins of Christianity and what it means. Thereafter the child may decide for himself or herself. I should regard it as a disaster if these clauses were undermined or removed.'

Mrs Shirley Williams was Secretary of State for Education in the Labour Government of the day and when she went to address the North of England Education Conference in Southport, Charles made sure she was aware of people's concern about religious education.

A favourite argument of the abolitionists has always been that because only a small percentage of the population attends a place of worship regularly, Christian teaching should therefore be dropped. Yet if that criterion were to be applied elsewhere, we should have to remove art and music from school curricula because only a small percentage of the population visits art galleries and concert halls.

Perhaps the most succinct and searching comment on the debate about religious education came in a letter to *The Daily Telegraph* in July 1976 from Richard Wilkinson, Headmaster of Scarborough College. His letter asked the simple question: 'Could there possibly be a case for teaching Christianity in schools because it is true?'

Another factor to be brought into the equation was how adherents of other religious faiths reacted to the suggestion that Judaism, Hinduism, Buddhism, Sikhism and Islam should be taught alongside Christianity? What about non-religious life stances coming under the umbrella of 'religious education'? Charles spoke to the parents of pupils who came from ethnic minorities. They themselves were predominantly Hindu or Muslim and they definitely did not want a British RE teacher from either a Christian or non-faith background trying to teach their children the Hindu or Muslim faith. They were happy for their children to be taught about Christianity at school and they as parents would attend to their religious upbringing outside school. The fact that up to 20% of the children at one of Charles Oxley's schools came from Hindu or Muslim backgrounds suggests their acceptance of Christian teaching, with the good behaviour and high standards to which it should lead.

Charles would not deny that there was a place for the study of other world religions, and for ideologies such as communism, nationalism, humanism and capitalism, but that place was not in RE lessons. Sixth Form General Studies classes could profitably study them once they had a solid grounding in the faith which has been a major influence on the social, moral, political and educational development of Britain.

How could school pupils be expected to understand the poetry of Milton if his biblical allusions were foreign to them? How would a child reading *The Merchant of Venice* have a reference point for the phrase 'a Daniel come to judgement' unless he knew more about Daniel than his visit to the lions' den—or maybe not even that?

A leader in *The Daily Telegraph* of June 23rd 1976 brought warm applause from Charles and his fellow-campaigners:—

> If there is still a Church Militant, then certain of what should be its crack regiments are showing a marked tendency to fraternise with other forces, not all of them on the same side. One by one, various important corps are—in varying degrees—opting for an end to the present statutorily-decreed Christian bias in State religious education: the British Council of Churches, the Religious Education Council, and now the Free Church Federal Council. They are marching alongside the British Humanist Association—apparently unworried by the fact that Humanists have a long-term war aim which is broadly inimical to that of Christians...

Charles took up the military metaphor in his letter of thanks to the editor:—

> The Christian Church in this country has laid down the sword of the Spirit, which is the word of God (it is too heavy); it has mislaid its shield of faith; it has taken off its helmet of salvation (too small now); it has unfastened its breastplate of righteousness (too tight); and it has been caught with its trousers down by the British Humanist Association.
>
> By showing all the fighting qualities expected of Christian soldiers, the British Humanist Association is within sight of victory in its determined and daring campaign to rid the schools of Christian education as far as possible...

If Charles had still been alive in June 1990, his response to a report by the Association of Christian Teachers might well have been 'I told you so.' It criticised the multi-faith approach to religious education, which was now widespread, claiming that it caused confusion among children and might even undermine personal religious belief. Tracing the problem back to the 1970s, the report said that 'many Christians felt, or were made to feel, a strong sense of guilt about their own faith, about the previous place of Christianity and the faith-building role of RE. This led to a boom in interesting teaching materials on various world religions, but to a neglect of Christianity.'

In some schools, teachers who followed Muslim, Sikh or Hindu religions were welcomed whereas committed Christians had been treated with suspicion and even hostility.

'When six major religions are presented equally with all their diversity, disagreement and mutually exclusive claims, the child may well consider that they are all equally irrelevant.' Presenting faiths as alternative paths to the same end might appear a way of avoiding disputes over exclusive religious truth, but there was a danger of 'devaluing the distinctive nature of each religion.'

§

IT WAS NOT ONLY in his schools that Charles Oxley sought to teach the Bible and its truth. For some years he organised the Liverpool branch of the London Bible College, which in due course became the Liverpool Bible College. Mainly through evening classes, students followed courses leading to fully accredited certificates and diplomas in Biblical Studies and Theology.

He was concerned, though, at the increasing liberalisation of courses in Theology in universities and colleges generally. He knew of too many keen Christians who had undertaken such courses with a living personal faith and emerged at the end—sometimes leaving before the end—with faith undermined and scepticism encouraged about the validity of the biblical text. Charles therefore approached a number of conservative evangelical Bible scholars to gain their support for a brainchild of his—the Examining Board for Biblical and Religious Studies.

His vision for the EBBRS was that it would span the full age and ability ranges, enabling students in schools, evening classes and Bible colleges to pursue courses in knowledge of the Bible and its application to the problems of daily living. He worked with great zeal to promote EBBRS courses through Christian magazines and Bible colleges, and also to gain accreditation with the Department of Education and Science. He hoped to counter the declining number of committed Christians going for training as RE teachers by establishing the principle of RE teacher training in Bible colleges.

In a meeting with a DES official and two men from HM Inspectorate, he put forward a definite proposal for an RE teaching diploma based on the Theology Certificate examination of the EBBRS linked with a course on education theory and practice. He knew of several Bible colleges that were willing to introduce such a course, but the men at the DES advised caution and suggested that he should approach local education authorities to see how they might react to the scheme.

Charles rarely bothered with holidays. While teachers generally took time at Easter or in the summer at least to wind down a little and recharge failing batteries, he saw these breaks from the daily routine of school as the ideal opportunities to throw himself into the mass of other activities to which he committed his time and energy.

Easter 1976 found him bringing together the Principals of fourteen Bible colleges in the UK to form an association. He had felt for some time that in the diversity of Christian opinion which appeared in the media, there ought at least to be some kind of platform for Bible scholars. The Principals gathered for a two-day conference at Scarisbrick Hall and found considerable unanimity on several issues. They were persuaded of the value of forming the Association of Bible College Principals and decided to appoint a secretary. Charles made the mistake of slipping out of the conference room to attend to some arrangements for refreshments, because when he returned, he found he had been proposed, seconded and appointed! He therefore represented the twenty-five members of the Association for the next five years and had the opportunity to travel to the continent two or three times a year to serve on the European Evangelical Accreditation Council, which operated under the auspices of the World Evangelical Fellowship. He found it both instructive and encouraging to meet with like-minded college principals from West Germany and other European countries.

His own biblical scholarship was immense. I once asked him a question about a fairly remote character in the Old Testament. In the next ten minutes he gave me a superbly clear and concise outline of the whole Old Testament in order to help me to see where and how this character fits into the total picture. And all from memory, with no need of reference to any book.

This vast knowledge of the Bible had contributed to Charles' MA degree, awarded by Liverpool University in 1976 for a 100,000-word thesis on Figurative Language in the Old Testament.

Meanwhile, Charles was keen to obtain premises for the Liverpool Bible College and for other Christian activities. When a large Welsh Presbyterian Church building in Princes Road, Toxteth, was put up for sale, Charles went to have a look and was excited by its potential. The building was listed as being of architectural importance and Liverpool Corporation had spent £10,000 on cleaning the stonework. The Welsh-speaking congregation had dwindled to only ten people where there was seating capacity for 1,200; two other meeting rooms could each accommodate 400-500 people and the premises also offered a small hall, vestry, kitchen and residential accommodation for a caretaker. The pipe organ was reputed to be worth £50,000. The congregation wanted the building used for Christian purposes rather than being demolished or used as a warehouse.

Charles with Rachel and Muriel outside the Liverpool Philharmonic Hall after receiving his MA in Biblical Studies from the University of Liverpool.

The asking price was £50,000, but the trustees met to consider and accept Charles' offer of £25,000. He knew that there would need to be expenditure on redecorating some of the smaller rooms and in providing new furniture.

The Princes Park Christian Centre, as it came to be known, was close enough to the heart of Liverpool to suggest it might be useful in a variety of ways. In addition to Bible College classes, Charles envisaged gospel rallies, church conventions, conferences for youth leaders and Sunday School teachers, young people's rallies, workshops on moral issues, meetings to bring well-known preachers and Bible teachers, and seminars to relate biblical principles to social issues. Two church groups would continue to use the premises for their worship and fellowship gatherings. It would be a possible venue also for performances of choral and organ music.

In the year following the purchase of the building, Charles managed to put on some of the projects he had envisaged, aided by George Bowden, a Baptist minister he appointed as manager of the Centre. They had to overcome various unforeseen difficulties, however, and the Princes Park Christian Centre never reached the level of usefulness that Charles wanted to establish.

The following year, 1978, a Nurses' Training College along the road came up for sale; it was considerably smaller than the Centre, but it would serve his main purposes better and cost much less to run. With some feelings of regret, he therefore bought the College building and put the Centre up for sale at £30,000. He contacted various churches and Christian groups around the Merseyside area, but the only group remotely interested could offer no more than a thousand pounds.

Then suddenly the estate agents telephoned to say that a Christian group had offered to buy the Centre for the full asking price; Charles was delighted, of course, and told the agents to accept the offer. He was somewhat dismayed a little later to discover that the would-be purchasers were the Unification Church, better known as the 'Moonies'. Charles knew very little about them, as they had yet to make a major impact in Britain, but what he had heard suggested that they were not a group to whom he wanted to sell. His swift enquiries about them reinforced his initial doubts, so he again turned to the Christian community. He wrote to the Liverpool city's community development officer to see if the Council might be interested to buy the property for community use, but again the response was negative.

By now, word had gone speedily round the Christian grapevine that Charles Oxley was selling a church building to the Moonies. Not for the first time in his life, he received several letters and telephone calls—some of them anonymous—both complaining about the proposed sale and vilifying him personally.

The Unification Church group were pressing him to exchange contracts and he spelled out his dilemma in a letter to the General Secretary of the Evangelical Alliance, Gordon Landreth, who had written to Charles expressing deep concern about a sale which would benefit an anti-Christian sect. Charles replied:—

I do not want to sell to the Unification Church, but if no evangelical or Christian body wants the premises, I cannot see that I should let it stand empty and have £30,000 of the Lord's money tied up in a building which is not being used for the purpose for which I bought it and which is costing a lot of money in heating and insurance, etc., simply to keep out a Christian cult with wrong doctrines. Otherwise, Christians generally should set up funds to prevent such organisations buying *any* premises, for after all it is only a building.

In the end, he decided not to sell to the Moonies, but it took another three years to sell the Centre, for £25,000—the amount Charles had paid for it five years earlier—to a group of African Christians.

The area in which both the Princes Park Centre and the Nurses' Home were situated—Toxteth—had been a district of elegant Victorian town houses even within the living memory of some local residents. When the wealthier families moved out to the suburbs, Toxteth, Liverpool 8, became a bedsit-land near the heart of the city, a honeycomb occupied by mainly immigrant families. The Liverpool Bible College now occupied the former Nurses' Home for three years, with increasing numbers of students and encouraging successes in examinations for the London University Bachelor of Divinity degree, the Cambridge Diploma and Certificate in Theology, as well as in the EBBRS courses.

The Toxteth riots of July 1981 brought progress to a sudden, sickening halt. Several cities suffered outbreaks of urban unrest, with attacks on police and property, and Liverpool 8 had its share of notoriety in one of the worst outbreaks of mob violence in recent British history. The Bible College building stood at the eye of the storm and all through the night Charles was on guard, embattled but defiant. The rioters had the gall to demand that he should let them use his premises as their headquarters. 'We've no time for Bible Colleges,' they snarled, though they probably had no idea what went on there. Charles refused to let them in. On reflection after the event, with not a single window broken in the College building, he could ascribe this fact only to God's protection of the property.

Across the road a cinema was reduced to rubble. To one side a bank was gutted; to the other a geriatric hospital had to be evacuated at 3 a.m. though the building remained undamaged. At the back of the College the hundred-year-old Racquet Club was left a blackened shell.

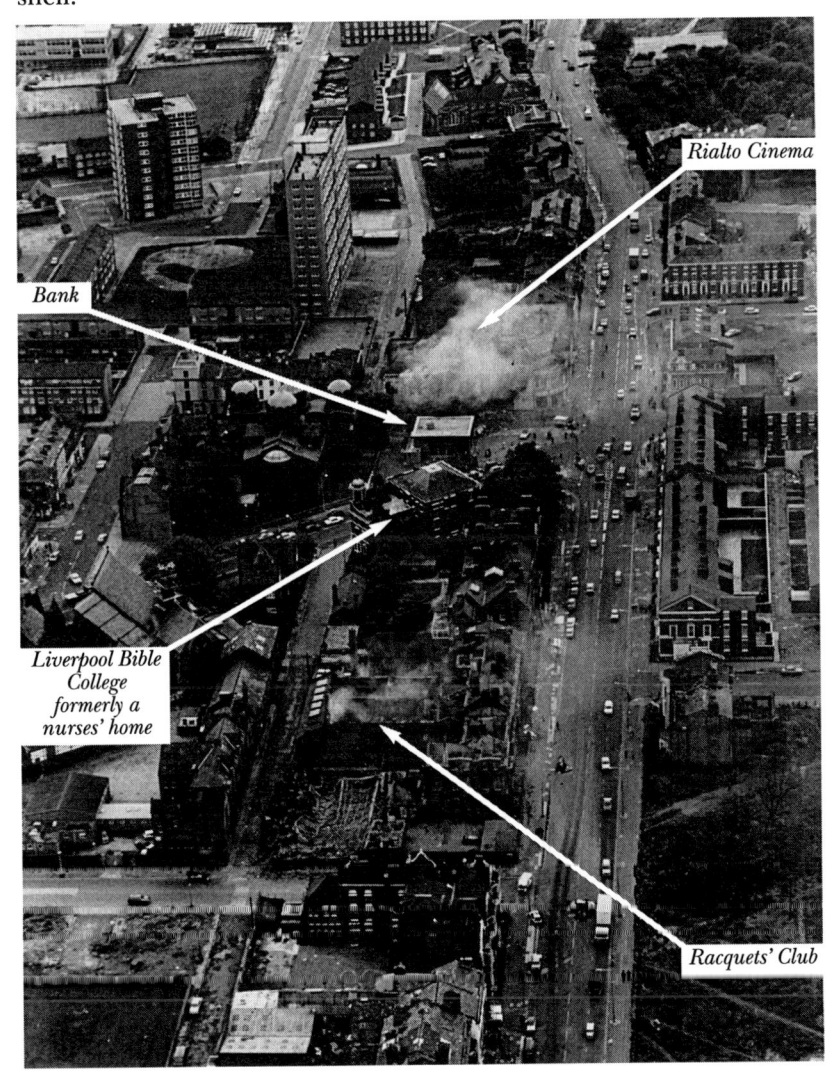

The aftermath of rioting in Toxteth, Liverpool, in 1981. Smoke can be seen rising from the shell of the gutted Rialto Cinema and 100-year-old Racquets Club. Despite the mayhem all around, the Liverpool Bible College building remained intact with not even a window broken.

Charles had positioned a fire extinguisher at the ready in every room, while he offered first aid, refreshments and a place of respite for battle-weary police officers. 'I couldn't believe what was happening,' he said. 'It was inexcusable that the police should be set up as aunt sallies to be bombarded with bricks and bottles thrown mostly by schoolchildren and teenagers. Groups of youths wandered about all night looking for trouble. I saw a girl of about 12 with four lads of 14 at three in the morning in Princes Road.'

Though shocked by the sheer physical horror of what he saw in Toxteth, Charles was not surprised that trouble had flared up. He had written to successive Home Secretaries and to the Chief Constable of Merseyside over several years to advise them of a serious breakdown of law and order in the Toxteth area. As a member of a Law and Order delegation he had met William Whitelaw at the House of Commons to express concern to the Home Secretary of the newly-elected Thatcher government. In a letter in August 1979 he pleaded with Mr Whitelaw to visit Liverpool 8. But the tide of lawlessness continued to build up until it flooded through Princes Road, Lodge Lane and Upper Parliament Street. In addition to the buildings that were completely destroyed, many shops had their windows smashed and their contents looted.

At the height of the rioting, Charles accompanied a local pastor, well respected in the area, to one of the nearby housing estates to plead with the rioters to end the violence, but without success. He was full of praise for this man's efforts to bring peace and also for the members of the Salvation Army whom he commended in a letter to the *Liverpool Daily Post*:—

> These Salvation Army personnel, men and young women, were out every night in the thick of the violence serving tea and offering their help to anyone in need. If the Christian Gospel which they preach were accepted and the self-sacrificing service which they practise were followed, the troubles of Toxteth would soon be resolved.

Although the Liverpool Bible College premises survived completely unscathed, Charles was realistic enough to see that its address— Toxteth, Liverpool 8—was hardly likely to attract droves of students, when the rioting had been reported around the world. After consulting the College's Advisory Council, he decided to move the work of the College to Scarisbrick Hall, where a wing of the main building could be set aside for lecture rooms and for student accommodation. Staff and students alike welcomed the move and once more the numbers of applications began to rise. Evening classes continued in Liverpool as well.

Charles' period of property-owning in Toxteth came to an end when he sold the former Nurses' Home to an independent Christian Fellowship. They had been using the basement of a Victorian house in the area to run a small Christian school. The larger premises would be far more suitable and Charles was happy to spread part of the payment over the next five years.

Chapter 9

SPY AMONG THE PAEDOPHILES

The headline writers of the popular press had a field day when the news broke of Charles Oxley's daring involvement with the child sex group, Paedophile Information Exchange. 'The Spy in the PIE', 'Undercover Crusader', 'Kiddie Sex Spy Tells All' trumpeted the news stories across the national dailies in September 1983. Yes, it was true—the Principal of three Christian schools and tireless campaigner for moral standards had infiltrated and exposed a particularly loathsome organisation.

The Paedophile Information Exchange had been founded in October 1974 by three members of the Scottish Minorities Group, who felt that there was a need in Britain for those people who were attracted—sexually and otherwise—to youngsters below the age of about seventeen. PIE's original leaflet stated its aims:—

1. To clear away, where possible, the myths connected with paedophilia by various means, including the making public of scientific, sociological and similar information.

2. To give advice and counsel to those isolated or lonely because of their paedophile orientation.

3. To help those in legal difficulties concerning sexual acts with under-age partners that took place with the latter's consent.

4 To campaign, as members see fit, for the legal and social acceptance of paedophile love.
5 To provide a means whereby paedophiles might get in contact with each other.

The trail that led Charles to finding out about the PIE originated in his 'Jonathan Hope' column for the local newspaper, in which he commented from a Christian standpoint on topical issues. A reader had sent him a cutting about paedophile activity.

'I was horrified by what I read,' admitted Charles. 'I could not believe that men could be so wicked.'

He at once wrote an article denouncing the paedophiles, cutting through their high-sounding language to expose their depraved and sordid practices. His attack drew a reply from Tom O'Carroll, a publicity officer with the Open University, who was later jailed for paedophile activities. O'Carroll's letter was signed, 'Yours faithfully, p.p. Satan,' an appropriate summing up of the sick mentality of such people.

What also caught Charles' eye was the Post Office box number which the letter contained. Here was a possible key to gain access to a very secretive organisation, so he began to keep a close eye on media reports of paedophile activities. Just how far he should go in delving into this dark world became a matter for serious prayer and careful thought. Eventually, after discussing his plan only with Muriel at this stage, he decided to move into action.

He took the assumed name Dave Charlton (his father being David Charlton Oxley) and wrote under that name to Tom O'Carroll at the PO box number, expressing an interest in the Paedophile Information Exchange and asking for any literature they might like to send him. (Charles' Brethren upbringing had taught him to keep a clear conscience before God, so it was no light thing for him to deceive anyone with a false name. As it turned out, this was the only deception he used in all his dealings with PIE. 'I admit it was a deception,' he said, 'but it was the lesser of two evils.')

So began a correspondence which lasted for five years between 1976 and 1981. Dave Charlton's mail was addressed to an elderly relative in St Helens, who had strict instructions never to open it. Charles hoped to glean addresses and clues about PIE members, but they were very careful. Eventually, therefore, he decided that the only effective way to fight the evil was from the inside. Dave Charlton duly signed an application for membership, sent off his subscription and soon received his membership card, Number 608.

In 1981 Tom O'Carroll was arrested and jailed for his paedophile activities. PIE became cagey about putting members in touch with each other, but 'Dave' received copies of their magazines and, after he expressed his willingness to do typing, duplicating, or printing a membership list with his school computer, it was suggested that he might like to meet the executive committee. At this stage he did not wish to meet the whole committee but asked if he could meet one of its leading members, Peter Bremner. Accordingly, in May 1982, Charles set aside his normal garb of scholarly suit, white shirt, sober tie and white pocket handkerchief and donned his new persona as Dave Charlton in an open-necked shirt and casual trousers. He drove down to an address in Clapton in the east end of London, a dismal house of shabby furniture and stale tobacco smoke, with paedophile books and papers scattered about the back room.

This was the home of Roger Nash, or Peter Bremner as he was known among the paedophiles: a slightly built, pale-faced chain smoker with a permanently worried expression. He talked freely to 'Dave' about the activities of PIE and about the secretarial work which 'Dave' was willing to do. He told Bremner quite truthfully that he was a schoolmaster and taught Latin; access to his school's reprographic equipment would present no difficulty to him!

Bremner had gained a doctorate from London University on the effect of light on living organisms; a copy of the thesis was on a bookshelf in his home. On the same shelf stood a photograph of a dark-skinned boy of about twelve years of age. When 'Dave' asked if he was Indian, Bremner replied, 'No, he's German. Isn't he beautiful?'

Following that first meeting, 'Dave' was then invited to a PIE executive meeting six weeks later, this time in north London. Having already set foot in the lions' den, Charles knew the risks involved and was committed to going ahead. He had already taken the precaution of informing Scotland Yard of his intentions and had passed on copies of the vile magazines he had been sent through the post.

Nevertheless, further infiltration of PIE could turn out to be costly. If his membership of the group leaked out prematurely, his professional standing could well be irrevocably damaged. Muriel realised the danger to her husband's reputation. 'But he felt very strongly about anyone who would harm a child in any way. He felt it was the duty of anyone who worked with children to protect them from evils such as this.'

The other risk—to Charles' personal safety—caused Muriel, if not her husband, under-

Charles and Muriel outside Scarisbrick Hall about the time when he was infiltrating a paedophile group.

standable anxiety. 'If people are so despicable that they can do terrible things to children, what would they have done to my husband?' She told him as he set off for that first meeting not to eat or drink anything they gave him. 'I was just so scared he would be found out, and they might doctor any food or drink he was offered.' In the event, however, when grubby mugs of tea were passed round, Charles felt he should avoid drawing attention to himself by refusing one, so he drank it.

Only once at a London meeting did Charles feel uneasy about possible physical danger. One particular scoundrel looked evil enough to produce a knife at any moment. The rest of them Charles described as 'weedy wimps', none of them a match for a fit six-foot-four sixteen-stoner trained in unarmed combat during the war.

When he drove down to London for the first executive committee meeting, he parked a few streets away from the venue. Every time he drove down, he borrowed a different car, never his own, so as not to be traced by his number plate.

As the PIE members came into the room for the meeting, Charles noticed a plywood notice at the side of the fireplace: 'Capacity of this room is limited to 28 consenting boys'. The man who sat next to him was David Joy, a former maths teacher. During the meeting Joy produced a pencil drawing of his six-year-old daughter sitting naked with her knees drawn up, exposing her private parts which were drawn in great detail. He wanted the drawing to be printed in the PIE magazine *Magpie*, but his request was ignored. Unknown to Charles, Joy had a criminal record already for sexually assaulting three girls of six, seven and eight. He had also had a sexual relationship with his daughter, which he described as being like that of man and wife.

Charles took careful note of who was present at the PIE meetings, jotting down names and details for identification. A leader among them was Steven Smith, a security guard employed at the Home Office. He obtained material for *Magpie*, wrote articles himself and had much to do with the editorial side of the magazine. Described by Charles as 'jumpy, energetic and articulate', he spoke openly about his sexual activities with boys and was in favour of PIE putting members in touch with each other. Bremner disagreed because of legal dangers.

On his way to an executive committee meeting in July 1982 Charles had agreed to pick up David Joy, who lived in Loughborough, and take him to the London venue. Arriving early at the rendezvous, he realised that he had time to go to Joy's home address, but as he reached the house, it was evident that someone had found out about Joy's paedophile activities, because windows in the front and back had been smashed, causing Joy to move out. He told Charles that he had applied to be rehoused and had been given a flat overlooking a children's playground. 'They couldn't have found a better place for me,' grinned Joy, sending a cold shiver down Charles' spine.

During that July meeting, the members sat outside in the sunshine at the back of the house, each in turn telling the group whether they were heterosexual or homosexual paedophiles. When it came to Charles' turn, he simply said, 'Heterosexual', thereby keeping to his self-imposed rule of not telling a lie to gain information. The others then boasted of some of their depraved sex acts.

The more Charles became involved with PIE, the greater the risk of discovery, either by PIE members becoming suspicious and making enquiries about him, or by eager journalists who were also on the trail of the paedophiles. On one particular Sunday both these possibilities arose.

First of all, when Charles arrived at the expected venue for an executive committee meeting, he found that the date had been put back a week without anyone informing him. The minutes of the previous meeting had not reached him either, though he knew others had received theirs. Both facts could have had quite innocent explanations, but their coinciding made him wonder whether he was under suspicion.

Then, as he made his way from the meeting place towards the side street a few blocks away where he had parked, a photographer at the open first-floor window of a corner house took two photographs of him. He could have used a zoom lens but had waited until Charles was only five yards away. The man was clearly visible, his camera shutter too noisy. Charles went to the door of the house and asked to speak to the photographer, who came down to him.

'What's the idea of taking my photograph like that?' asked Charles.

'Oh, I wasn't taking you, mate,' the man replied, 'I was taking shots of the architecture of houses along the street.'

'Come off it, you took two close-ups of me, so why deny it?'

It transpired that the man was working for a Sunday newspaper and he admitted that he was on the paedophile story. Charles knew the journalist responsible for the investigation, so he telephoned him promptly and advised him to keep his photographer better hidden if the whole set-up was not to be disclosed prematurely.

The Paedophile Information Exchange had two hundred and forty-nine UK members at that time and Charles really needed to get his hands on the closely-typed nine-page membership list. Having proved his usefulness to the committee by the typing and photocopying he had been doing already, he was hopeful that they might trust him to do the job of re-typing the membership list at some point. However, during Any Other Business at one meeting, awkward questions were raised about security leaks, so much so that Charles felt they suspected him of having contacts in the press. Although they told him the date and place for the next meeting, he wondered whether they might switch the venue in order to see if any photographers turned up at the original one.

Charles had actually seen the membership list in the possession of Steven Smith. Knowing that Smith was going straight to a double shift on duty in the Home Office that night, Charles realised that he would still have the membership list with him in the large, square plastic bag in which he carried his PIE literature. As Charles drove home in the early hours of Monday morning, he decided to telephone his contact at Scotland Yard as early as possible, since it seemed a great opportunity to obtain the membership list from Smith's room at the Home Office. Later that day the Vice Squad did raid the office and found plenty of incriminating literature, though not, unfortunately, the membership list. In the end Charles was able to pass on the names of nine members, plus a dossier of evidence about PIE's activities. This, added to the obscene magazines sent to him through the post, gave scope for court action to follow.

In August 1982 PIE executive committee members positively identified Charles, in his absence, as the source of material appearing in a Sunday newspaper.

Scotland Yard had enough evidence to mount a convincing case against Peter Bremner, David Joy and Steven Smith. For a full year, however, the Director of Public Prosecutions refused all requests for proceedings. Then, in August 1983, there was a huge public outcry when three men sexually assaulted a small boy in Brighton and at last the DPP decided to act against PIE. Charles spent eight hours in the witness box at Bromley Magistrates Court and Bremner, Joy and Smith were committed for trial at the Old Bailey. The case came up in November 1984 and Charles spent his thirty-eighth wedding anniversary as chief prosecution witness against Bremner and Joy, Smith having fled the country while on bail.

Defence lawyers raised objections to each of the six women brought forward to serve on the jury, so that the trial was conducted with an all-male jury. To Charles' disgust and dismay, the two men were cleared of incitement to commit buggery, unlawful sex or indecent assault. They were each sentenced to six months in prison for sending obscene material through the post, and Joy was given eighteen months for publishing an obscene article.

Steven Smith was arrested in Holland, but when Britain applied for his extradition, the request was turned down. The Dutch judge commented that the law was different in the Netherlands and indeed only a few days earlier the Vatican had strongly criticised new Dutch legislation on pornography as being 'a crime against human dignity'.

Smith's escape from conviction brought a huge headline in the *Scottish Daily Record*, quoting the principal of Hamilton College: 'I'LL NAIL THIS SEX BEAST.' Charles was by no means satisfied that the job was done. 'Steven Smith is the worst offender of the lot,' he said. 'I will not rest until this filthy group has been wiped out.' He spent time and further effort in an already busy life to try and take matters further, only to be thwarted by legal niceties. He had some consolation seven years later when Steven Smith returned to Britain and was arrested for publishing an obscene magazine and sending it through the post, receiving an eighteen-month prison sentence after his trial at the Old Bailey. There had been times during the whole sordid business when he had felt like giving up, but he was constantly spurred on by words he had read in an issue of the paedophile publication *Magpie*: 'If a child has not had a sexual experience by the age of four, then it is too late.' He thought of his own grandchild, of the innocence of tiny boys and girls in the kindergarten of his schools, and the strength of his resolve flooded back.

One disturbing aspect of the PIE episode was the fact that Tom O'Carroll had been able to receive a paedophile book during a two-year sentence in Wandsworth Prison for conspiring to corrupt public morals. He had even written a 1,400-word review of the book, because Charles had typed a copy of it while doing his secretarial work for PIE. He wrote to the Home Secretary complaining that O'Carroll had access to paedophile literature while in prison. The Home Office at first denied it, but when Charles pressed the matter it was admitted that O'Carroll had been permitted 'a brief sight of one paedophile book before it was placed in his stored property.' Charles knew that this was less than accurate: O'Carroll must have studied the book at some length to be able to write a review of it.

In September 1982, soon after Charles' infiltration and exposure of PIE had become headline news, Tom O'Carroll wrote to *The Guardian* to try and play down what Charles' spying activities had achieved:—

> The only revelation seems to be that I received a book in Wandsworth Prison dealing with issues—(power, equality, consent, etc.)—raised by paedophilic relations, and that I wrote a review of it.
>
> Leaving aside the issue of prison censorship, Mr Oxley's case for making PIE an illegal organisation appears to be based solely on a wish to suppress the legitimate expression of ideas. PIE is not, after all, a terrorist organisation. We use no bullets or bombs. Nor has Mr Oxley's extensive spying disclosed illegality of *any* kind.
>
> Is PIE then to be suppressed merely to appease the Whitehouse faction's lust for 'moral' hegemony? Is there to be created a minority unique in society, who alone could be harassed and punished simply for organising so as to express their views?

Charles' reply aimed to blow away the smokescreen of claimed respectability and to expose the sordid depravity of paedophile thinking and activity:—

> Tom O'Carroll's attempt to pose as the leader of a harmless pressure group concerned with 'the legitimate expression of ideas' is as false as his attempt to minimise the amount of information I have obtained about his organisation's activities.
>
> Over a period of six years, I discovered through careful reading of all publications, including the magazine for members only, through personal correspondence with seven members of the executive, through conversations with leading members and through attendance at meetings of the executive committee that the organisation is led by men who preach sexual activity with young children and practise what they preach. Some have boasted of their actions in my hearing.
>
> O'Carroll describes my desire for the physical safety and moral wellbeing of children as a 'lust for moral hegemony'. Rather that than a sexual lust by pathetic perverts for boys and girls aged four and five.

Despite Charles' efforts in exposing PIE and seeing two of its members prosecuted with a measure of success, he was far from satisfied with the law relating to sexual abuse of children. There was nothing to prevent paedophiles re-grouping under another title to indulge in their perversions and spread their ideas. The battle must transfer to Parliament, so that any such organisation could be proscribed. The Home Office was not inclined to act speedily on the matter and without Government backing there seemed little hope of changing the law.

Nevertheless, Charles saw the need to maintain the impetus which the PIE case had provided. He contacted sympathetic MPs to enlist their support, wrote to the ten people whose names topped the poll for Private Members' Bills and wrote to the Home Secretary. Geoffrey Dickens, the MP for Littleborough and Saddleworth, had for some time been a comrade-in-arms, even if his style did not always tally with Charles Oxley's. Mr Dickens caused an uproar in the Commons in 1981 when he used the protection of parliamentary privilege to name a former British diplomat as a paedophile. He now approached the Home Secretary, Leon Brittan, to urge Government action against paedophile groups.

Charles' letter to the Home Secretary presented a cogent argument for a change in the law:—

> Over the ten years of the organisation's existence, the leaders have vigorously pursued their aims by publishing a magazine called *Magpie*; by addressing meetings of students at universities and colleges; by distributing their literature in homosexual clubs, left-wing political clubs and bookshops, and in public libraries. The executive committee of nine members meets monthly to review progress and to plan new ways of promoting adult/child sexual activity. Enclosed are some stickers used in one of their recruitment drives. They give advice to members on ways of seducing children as young as three or four years of age, recommending the practice of hanging around children's playgrounds in public parks and leisure centres, and making friends with families with the object of gaining the parents' confidence to allow them to take children on outings or to allow them to 'baby sit'.
>
> I am aware that there is great reluctance to proscribe an organisation which claims merely to be trying to educate the public and reform the law, because of the great value of freedom of speech, but there are some essential differences between normal pressure groups and PIE and there are compelling reasons for the proscription of PIE.
>
> The main and crucial difference is that PIE wants to decriminalise a most appalling crime, perpetrated against the most vulnerable

members of society, namely small children, exposing them to long-term physical, psychological and emotional harm. The corrupting nature of the harm done is likely to trap the child into continued sexual perversion into adult life, so putting other small children at risk. The sexual abuse of children is worse than rape in several respects, mainly that a child is less likely to recover psychologically.

If two or three hundred men formed themselves into an organisation for the legalisation of rape, recruiting convicted rapists as life members free of subscriptions, openly publishing propaganda to make rape legally and socially acceptable, publicly denouncing laws forbidding rape, their activities would be such an affront to decency and such a danger to society, that they would have to be stopped. But PIE has been allowed to pursue for ten years aims which are of the same character and to use the same methods as those envisaged above.

As I see it, there is a choice of freedoms here: either the freedom of vicious perverts to propagate their perversions or the freedom of children to play in public parks free from danger of sexual abuse, plus the freedom of parents and grandparents from the fear of such molestation of their children and grandchildren.

Among the compelling reasons for the immediate proscription of PIE is that persons who organise themselves to campaign for the acceptance of adult/child sexual relations represent a serious danger to small children and the Government has a clear duty to protect children against such dangers.

Also, the activities of PIE and similar organisations with the same aims represent a danger to society, and the Government has a clear duty to protect society from such a corrupting influence and to express the strong disapproval and special abhorrence felt by the public at the prospect of adult/child sexual relations.

Furthermore, if Parliament does *not* proscribe PIE and organisations with its aims, the inaction will be seen as tacit acceptance of PIE's credibility and as a recognition of PIE's cause and it will give great encouragement to other pressure groups who are campaigning for the lowering of the 'age of consent'.

Since the publication of the press reports on the conviction of two of the leading members of PIE on the lesser charges and their acquittal on the more serious charge of incitement, I have been inundated with letters from ordinary decent citizens who are horrified that such an organisation is allowed to exist. Most letters are from mothers and grandmothers.

I have also received several letters and telephone calls from mothers whose children have been sexually abused, but who have not reported the offence for fear of publicity or fear of reprisal, or because of a lack of faith in the judicial system to punish criminals.

You, Sir, will know how difficult it is to prove incitement to sexual crimes, hence the acquittal of men whom I knew to be guilty of such offences. I sat and listened to members of the executive committee of PIE boasting to one another of their 'successes'.

With great respect, Sir, may I urge you most earnestly to initiate or give Government support to legislation to proscribe organisations whose aims include the legal and social acceptance of adult sexual relations with children under sixteen years of age.

Charles sent this letter in 1984. It was not until 1989, a year and a half after his death in 1987, that the Children Act completed its passage through all stages of Parliament: it dealt with a wide range of issues affecting children's well-being and provided for stern punishment for those advocating or indulging in sexual abuse of children.

Not everybody approved of Charles' infiltration and exposure of the Paedophile Information Exchange: the grounds of his home at Tower College were always easily accessible to those determined to get in, and one morning when the press publicity was at its height, the family woke to find obscenities daubed in white all over the school minibus and classroom windows.

Perhaps the most touching tribute to Charles' daring undercover work came in a letter from a teenage boy who, as a boarder at Scarisbrick Hall, had more than once been hauled before the Principal for his wrongdoings. He wrote: 'We may not have agreed on many things, but I would like to congratulate you and thank you for what you have done. I am very glad that these perverted men were convicted, and just wish that they were dealt with a lot more severely. I personally couldn't have done what you did, as I couldn't hide my disgust. I am very glad you did it as I have a 10-year-old sister and some day may have my own children.'

Chapter 10

NEEDS OF NORTH INDIA

Charles first took an interest in India at the age of sixteen when he read of the exploits of William Carey and C T Studd. Then it was during his time in the Merchant Navy that he began to see something of the needs of the vast sub-continent for himself. Long days and weeks waiting for his ship to be loaded with cargo in Bombay harbour gave him ample time and opportunity to explore the city and visit outlying areas.

Years later, in October 1963, he was invited to attend the opening of Delhi Bible Institute; it had been set up to be a strategic training centre for Christian pioneers in evangelism and church-planting in Northern India. Much of the missionary work in the past had been centred in the South and along the East coast, leaving the North largely untouched. The day of the European missionary seemed to be over. One man from Belfast had laboured for twenty-five years in Bangalore without seeing a single Hindu converted to Christ.

With a Bible Institute set up in Delhi, indigenous Christian workers from the South, whose mother tongue was Malayalam, could learn Hindi and receive periodic Bible training. They could then

Charles, back centre, committed much time, energy and money to encourage young men to spread the Christian gospel in Northern India

move out from the capital into areas where as yet the gospel of Jesus Christ was unknown.

During his two-month visit in 1963—immediately after completing the deal to buy Scarisbrick Hall—Charles was a principal speaker at a conference of fifty full-time Indian Christian workers. The strategy for outreach and church-planting was explained to these men, who responded with eagerness to the challenge. They were mostly in their twenties and thirties, and they had given up worthwhile careers in the South to be part of this pioneering work.

'However much they learnt from me, I am sure I learnt far more from them,' said Charles. 'They taught me what it is to give yourself in loving service to the Lord. They knew they would face hardship and they were ready and willing to do so with joy. There was so little financial support from their home assemblies, but they had absolute faith that the Lord would supply their needs. They also showed me what it is to launch out in new ventures even when they were fully stretched.'

It was at the opening of the Delhi Bible Institute that Charles first met MA Thomas, a man who is probably the nearest Indian equivalent to a Charles Oxley in his zeal to set up Christian schools and Bible colleges. He had come from the South of India in 1960 to do pioneer Christian work with his wife and three other men in the city of Kota in the state of Rajasthan. Through distribution of tracts and other literature, they had begun to make an impact on their locality, so much so that they were attacked by angry mobs who burst into their home and burned Bibles, tracts and hymn books. Undeterred, they set up worship meetings and began to establish a church in Kota. After a year, Thomas's co-workers moved on to other areas to start new works.

Over the next twenty years Charles was to pay a further nine visits to India, staying mainly with 'Brother Thomas' and his family, but also spending time visiting churches, schools and Bible colleges set up and staffed by other Christians. He had particular admiration for men who had gone alone into towns where there was not a single Christian and, in spite of sometimes ruthless opposition, had openly proclaimed the gospel, won converts and set up church assemblies.

During his first visit in 1963, Charles had to put up with some rather trying circumstances in which to prepare his addresses for the conference and also write the correspondence course lessons he had been asked to prepare for use by students at the Institute. He stayed with a British missionary family and in one of his letters home described each of the four children. The eldest was 'a bossy beggar and roars at his sisters all the time'; one daughter was 'a petted little things who won't eat her meals and cries nearly all the time'; another girl was 'terribly aggressive ... and fights with everyone'; and 'the baby does a fair amount of crying and squawking, too.' He referred kindly to the parents and was very grateful to be able to stay with the family. His only other hardship worth mentioning was that his bed was very hard 'and my feet stick out over the end nearly through the door'. Indian bed-builders clearly do not have to provide very often for men of six feet four inches!

Brother MA Thomas and family at a school he and Charles set up

During a visit to India at Christmas in 1975 (three weeks holiday at his own schools), Charles kept a very detailed diary of his activities and impressions. He stayed mainly with the Thomas family in Kota, but visited other towns, spoke in churches, Sunday Schools, day schools, colleges—a total of twenty-one addresses in fourteen days. He was also working at that time on a commentary on the book of Ruth as his contribution to *A Bible Commentary for Today*. (The book was edited by eminent evangelical scholars GCD Howley, FF Bruce and HL Ellison: it brought together the work of many leading Brethren men in a large single-volume commentary, published by Pickering and Inglis in 1979.)

Charles had given Brother Thomas the first £5 towards building a day school in Kota; now, four years later, he was able to see what had been achieved, including a fine building with ten classrooms, a playing field and plans to admit boarders as the school continued to grow. Brother Thomas was troubled by a duodenal ulcer and within two days of Charles' arrival he had to go into hospital. When the doctor ordered a blood transfusion of seven or eight pints, Brother Thomas cheerfully asked eight of those visiting him from the Bible school if they would donate one pint each and they, equally cheerfully, agreed to do so. Two days later he discharged himself from hospital at 6 a.m. so as to supervise arrangements for the school carol service. Not for him the well-intentioned advice of his doctor: 'No hurry, no worry, no curry!'

Some of Charles' diary entries make fascinating reading. Monday, 22nd December, for example, records a visit to Lakheri:—

Left by motor-cycle pillion for station—a hair-raising ride. I was sitting side-saddle and felt very insecure; I was holding a case and my Bible in one hand and held on with the other. There was one foot-rest, but I had difficulty in keeping the other foot off the ground. Because we would travel back from Lakheri at night I was advised to take a heavy coat. It was brilliant sunshine, about 85 degrees. I must have looked odd but no-one seemed to notice. Pedestrians, children, cows, goats, pigs and dogs wander about the unmade bumpy narrow road. Other motorbikes, cycles and three-wheeler taxis fly about with complete disregard for any highway code.

We arrived at the Kota station, met about 14 brothers and sisters and awaited the train—it was not too crowded but very dirty with peanut shells all over the floor. It was hot and the view over the plain with the limestone hills was very impressive. The train stopped at five small stations travelling north. We got down at Lakheri and travelled by an ancient bus about one mile to the school along an unmade road.

After a look round the school, there were refreshments, a Christmas display by the children, and Charles gave a Christmas message to the three hundred people present.

> We had a meal. The brothers sat round the table and the sisters sat on a form by the wall. They all eat with their hands. They thoughtfully gave me a spoon. They are messy eaters but were in a happy mood—talking all the time and laughing heartily...
>
> We waited for the bus. It came at 10.30 p.m. We rattled along the unmade road in the dark but everyone was happy. We waited in the station waiting room and had great difficulty getting on the train. The doors cannot be opened from the outside and the people inside won't open the doors because it is so crowded. Brother Sergis climbed in through a window and opened the door an inch or two. It was jammed by a steel box. I bashed the door against the box until it was wide open and pushed about eight brothers and sisters onto the train over six or seven people on the floor. We all got in. The others by another door.
>
> A big argument arose between Brother Sergis and four soldiers who occupied the whole compartment lying on the two upper and lower berths; the sisters were standing in the corridor. They said it was a reserved compartment for the military. Brother Sergis went in the compartment—and I followed him in case he should get into a fight. They shouted for three-quarters of an hour. I didn't know what they were saying but was ready to do what was necessary.
>
> Tuesday, 12.30 a.m. We arrived at Kota where the argument continued. A lance corporal complained to the station-master. He was soon told that no compartments were reserved for the Army except officers and if he didn't get back on the train the station-master would report him to his Colonel. Everyone seemed to take this upset as quite normal.
>
> The entrance to the station was covered in blankets with sleepers inside completely covered. I don't know how or what they breathe.
>
> We returned by motor-cycle to Brother Thomas' house at 1 a.m. I did not feel tired so did some 'Ruth' until 3.30 a.m. A dog yapped the whole time and mosquitoes buzzed about.

Charles' experience of carol singing in India was also a novelty. Late on Christmas Eve he went with some of the brothers round several houses, singing carols and choruses as well as 'We wish you a merry Christmas'. One of the brothers would pray for the family of the house, who in turn would bring out something to eat—a greasy fritter, a spiced bun, or some peanuts. Some would bring a very milky cup of tea—also greasy. They ended up in a brother's house eating curried eggs before going to bed at 1.30 a.m., but again Charles did not sleep well because of a dry cough, barking dogs and other night noises.

On Christmas Day, Charles and Brother Thomas both spoke in a morning service lasting three and a half hours, then went to the school for a lunch consisting of chicken and mutton with mountains of rice.

'They are dreadfully messy eaters,' he recalled. 'They scoop everything in their right hand and pick chicken bones off large leaves from the teak trees. Afterwards they threw the leaves to some pigs in the road outside. Then they washed their hands under a stand tap in the playground or from a metal tumbler. They rubbed their teeth, snorked and snorted and spat on the earth playground, and blew their noses out on the ground. They saw me constantly blowing my nose in a handkerchief and putting it in my pocket and probably thought it to be a disgusting habit!'

At an Indian orphanage he helped to establish, Charles enjoying a meal with some of the children and making no sartorial concessions to heat or humidity.

It was after this 1975 visit that Charles set up 'Needs of North India', a charitable scheme whereby Christians in British churches, in Bible classes or even as individuals could sponsor a student to train at Delhi Bible Institute for full-time Christian ministry in the unevangelised towns and cities of the North of India. By giving £10 per month for twenty months, they could see a student through his course, and they would have a photograph and information from the student so as to be able to take a personal interest in his welfare and progress. A separate fund for occasional gifts was also set up to help meet urgent needs of individual students.

Charles publicised this scheme in *The Harvester*, a magazine read by Brethren people, and there was some response from local assemblies and a few individuals. Yet in continuing correspondence with his growing numbers of contacts in India, it is clear that the bulk of the money which Charles sent over came from his own pocket. He would hardly ever write a letter to India without enclosing at least a small amount. If it came from another person or group he would remind the Indian brother receiving the gift that he should write to the donors. Perhaps some of those brothers were too busy or just forgetful of such etiquette, but the scheme did not grow to the extent that Charles would have wished.

Charles grew to hate the British way of celebrating Christmas, with so much commercialism and so little Christ. It is hardly surprising to find that he preferred to spend Christmas in India if he could. He went there again in December 1978 for a visit of two weeks. Fog and a strike by baggage handlers at Heathrow delayed his flight; yet, despite arriving in Delhi at 7.40 a.m., he then endured a lengthy train journey to Kota so that he could speak at two afternoon carol services—attended by a total of a thousand people—and address the Bible College students in the evening.

The night of Christmas Eve he recalled vividly for the amount of time he spent swatting all the mosquitoes which had conspired to stop him sleeping. Nonetheless, he spoke at the three-hour Christmas morning service in the assembly at Kota; then, after a communal lunch with the church people, he was once again a pillion on Brother Thomas' motorbike for the journey to Kota military camp. The congregation of seven hundred for the special Christmas service included the Brigadier, the Colonel, their wives, the officers and men and families. Charles' evening was no relaxation, either—leading the Bible College prayer meeting and doing some writing before he eventually went to bed.

As he visited various towns and their Christian assemblies, he was again impressed by the dedication which so many of these Indian brothers had shown in going to hostile areas to set up a new Christian witness. It was all the more saddening, therefore, when in correspondence the following year (1979) he found that these same pioneering men were not seeing entirely eye to eye, as has sometimes been the case throughout Christian history from Paul and Barnabas onwards. The way the Delhi Bible Institute was being run caused one split; disapproval by a few men of Brother Thomas' methods caused another; there may even have been some jealousy. Whatever the roots of the problems, Charles continued to support the North India work, mainly through Brother Thomas, but also directly to other men in key towns and cities.

Near the end of 1980 Charles promised to pay half the cost of the land and half the cost of the building for a new school in Faridabad, a dormitory town twenty-five miles from Delhi with a fast rail link. He became excited at the prospect of setting up a Christian school in India along similar lines to the two he had already established in England. The emphasis would again be on high academic standards, with excellent facilities, exemplary behaviour by the pupils and high qualifications among the staff. The main hindrance was the reluctance of the Indian government to give consent for the purchase of the land.

In the previous five years the evangelistic thrust into Northern India had produced twenty-seven new churches, three Bible Colleges, twenty-two day schools and two orphanages—one in Delhi and one in Kota. The momentum must be maintained and Faridabad offered great potential. Charles visited India again over Christmas and the New Year of 1980/81. Soon afterwards, though, his financial resources were being overstretched by heavy losses on Liverpool Bible College, so he was unable to send money as readily as before to meet the needs in India.

He was scheduled to travel again to India in March 1984, but in the end was unable to do so because of the pressure of work at home (by then he had opened a third school in Britain). Later that year

Brother Thomas made his second visit to England, staying with Charles and Muriel at Tower College and enjoying the opportunity for long conversations on their many mutual interests and hopes for the future. During his visit Brother Thomas was interviewed on BBC Radio Merseyside about his work in India. He visited all three of Charles' schools and when the pupils heard about the extent of his work, they were particularly challenged by the thought of children in orphanages, especially as some came from leper colonies. Charles had no difficulty in encouraging the pupils to raise money for the 'Needs of North India' charity. Tower College and Hamilton College between them produced a total of £4,000, which Charles and Muriel made up to £5,000. Scarisbrick Hall were already committed to supporting another charity for that school term, but later they also sent a substantial sum.

Two years after Charles' death in 1987, an appeal came from Brother Thomas for funds to extend the orphanage in Kota. The pupils of Scarisbrick Hall School responded with almost £2,000 as a memorial to Charles' long-standing support for Christian work in North India.

MA Thomas recalls Charles as 'a strong and brave soldier of Jesus Christ ... His teaching and pleasant smiling face was a great encouragement in my life. He was never afraid of hard work and hard life in India.' If India provided Charles with an escape route from the horrors of an English Christmas, it certainly was not escapism either for him or for those with whom he laboured. He was committed to the spread of the gospel and the building of God's Kingdom in Northern India, and he was constantly challenged by the self-sacrifice of young men who gave themselves wholeheartedly to evangelistic outreach and Bible training.

In fact, Charles always took a personal delight in spending time with eager young Christians; he had so much to impart from his own deep knowledge of the Bible, particularly the Old Testament, where his own degree studies had been centred. For many years he gave a full day in his busy schedule to lecture to the students at Capernwray Bible School, near Carnforth in north Lancashire. Billy Strachan, the college principal, became a good friend of Charles and Muriel, and it was he who was entrusted to lead the graveside service at Charles' funeral. Each year he would write to invite Charles to spend a day at

Capernwray and Charles would readily agree to tackle some Bible theme. In later years, however, he changed tack, feeling that he should alert these keen young Christians to the needs of the nation as he observed the spiritual and moral decline.

The thrust of his message was that the media, the law-makers, the educationalists and even the Church had retreated from long-established Bible-based principles to leave the people of Britain in a moral wasteland. He would never leave it at that, though, because he remained optimistic for the future advance of God's Kingdom as long as there were men and women like himself who had the vision and the vigour to restore Christian standards.

The Capernwray students always responded well to whatever challenge Charles brought them and they clearly enjoyed his visits. One year they found out that the day of his visit was also his birthday, so they gave him a birthday present, sang 'Happy Birthday to you' and generally made a fuss of him. He had nowhere to hide... and thoroughly enjoyed the fun of the occasion.

Chapter 11

SCHOOL NUMBER THREE IN SCOTLAND

To set up one independent school would satisfy many people; to start a second and larger school as well would stretch most people to the limit; even to think of adding a third would give anybody nightmares. Anybody, that is, apart from Charles and Muriel Oxley.

Muriel herself had some misgivings about the new venture. 'My husband was already turned sixty and was involved in so many campaigns and committees that I really thought he would be taking on too much. Not only that—Hamilton College is two hundred and five miles from our home at Tower College and it would mean so many long journeys there and back to see the school established.'

Yet curiously it was Muriel who sparked Charles' imagination about a third school. She and Rachel had attended a believers' baptism in Hamilton and when they returned home they described to Charles where it had taken place—in the heated indoor swimming pool of a large modern College of Education which was closing down. Charles was soon on the telephone to confirm the closure and sale of the property in 1982 by sealed offer. No hint of a price was given, except to say that it had been built for £2 million in the 1960s and was now valued at £6 million!

A conducted tour of the College almost took Charles' breath away. The main block offered teaching facilities for nine hundred students on four floors. Separate residential blocks, which he would not want, could accommodate six hundred. The fifty-one acre site included extensive playing fields lying within the loop of Hamilton racecourse. He was shown the thousand-seater auditorium, lecture rooms, science laboratories, music and art rooms, two gyms, a large sports hall and the swimming pool. Knowing that his company reserves could not stretch far beyond £250,000, Charles felt a little uneasy as he was plied with tea and scones in the Manager's office.

Hamilton College. Built for £2 million and said to be worth £20 million, the four-storey building, with its playing fields encircled by Hamilton racecourse, was bought by the Oxleys for £270,000.

He had no doubts about the premises—they were absolutely perfect for a school. But the distance from home ... and the colossal overheads ... and would the Scots accept the Oxley educational philosophy? Could a school possibly maintain financial viability or would he be overreaching himself and causing the collapse of Christian Schools Ltd and the closure of the two successful schools in England?

These were the big questions which Charles and Muriel brought before God in prayer. They were mature enough in their walk with God to see the danger of going beyond faith into presumption, so they had to have it very clearly from God if it was right to go ahead, just as they had found God making the way clear twenty years earlier though on a tenth of the scale financially. Yes, it would be splendid to establish a school in the town where Charles' maternal grandparents had first met, at an open-air evangelistic meeting, and where they had first set up home. It was also in Hamilton that Charles' mother Margaret had been born.

But surely there was hardly a chance that their bid of £270,000 for the main teaching block and playing fields would be accepted, was there?

In May 1982 that was the offer that Charles and Muriel put in and, much to their surprise and delight, it received official acceptance! Solicitors got to work on the details until, in October, a date was set for the last chance to 'resile' (a Scottish word meaning: withdraw). Initial excitement had diminished only as apprehension increased. Charles had arranged to telephone his Glasgow solicitor by 11 p.m. on the fateful day.

During that evening, he was addressing about four hundred people in a church hall in Preston who were mounting a campaign against two sex shops which had recently opened in the Lancashire town. After the meeting Charles had an interview for local radio. Noticing that the sound engineer had a Scottish accent, he half-jokingly asked if he thought Hamilton would be a suitable place for a Christian independent school. The man said he had no idea, but he did give Charles the name and telephone number of a senior schools inspector. When Charles rang this man at 10 p.m., his heart began to beat faster when he realised that he was talking to a highly respected member of a Brethren assembly near Hamilton! Yes, said the man, a Christian school in the area was desperately needed; yes, he had no doubt that it would be widely welcomed and well supported.

When Charles had driven back to St Helens from Preston, Muriel told him that a man from another Brethren assembly near Hamilton had telephoned, having heard about the plans for a new school, and wanted to enrol his three grandchildren. Both these contacts seemed to confirm the conclusion they had reached, so just before 11 p.m. Charles rang the Glasgow solicitor to give the final go-ahead.

When the news broke that Hamilton College was to be sold to an English educational entrepreneur at a price nowhere near the value of the property, to open an independent school, the howls of protest came loud and long. Hamilton had a Labour-controlled Council and a Labour MP, George (now Lord) Robertson, who questioned the sale in the House of Commons. Journalists flocked to the College and Charles made the most of all this free publicity from radio, television and press coverage.

School Number Three in Scotland

Applications from teachers came pouring in—about three hundred of them—months before the school was to open. Nearly half of these came from newly-qualified Bachelors of Education, whose standard of spelling horrified Charles. Most of the rest were from teachers finding it tough in state schools. The gold amongst the dross was the fifteen well-qualified, experienced teachers who had a clear Christian commitment and shared the educational aspirations of Charles Oxley. He appointed eleven of them even though, at that stage, applications from teachers outnumbered those from parents who wanted to enrol their children by about three to one!

Meanwhile, the furore over the sale of the College continued. How could a building erected for £2 million of public money in the mid-sixties, and now reckoned to be worth £20 million replacement cost, be sold for little more than a quarter of a million? That question came before the House of Commons Committee of Public Accounts on 16th November 1983. It transpired that the Scottish Education Department had tried to find other publicly-funded bodies who might be interested in the College, but with no success. When the College was offered for sale in late 1981 and early 1982, four offers were received but they all required planning permission and development grants for change of use. The local Council would consider the conversion of the halls of residence into housing, but the main block could only be used for educational purposes.

Hamilton College opened in 1983 and is now run by a separate company.

In the absence of other interest in the site, and because it would be very costly to maintain an empty building (an estimated £325,000 per year), the authorities recommended acceptance of the two offers—£410,000 for the halls of residence and £270,000 for the main block plus playing fields. The Scottish Education Department was criticised by the Public Accounts Committee for its handling of the sale: '... SED failed to ensure that everything possible was done, particularly through determined exploration of the possibilities for alternative use or development, to market the property adequately.'

Meanwhile the new school was already in operation. With his usual keen business sense, Charles had delayed occupation of the premises until 1st July 1983 so as to avoid paying rates unnecessarily; he and Muriel therefore had less than two months to get everything ready for the first intake of pupils. They made extensive internal structural alterations, redecorated many areas, put in furniture and science laboratory equipment, installed books and stationery, and arranged a six-coach transport service.

On the first day of the new term, 27th August 1983, two hundred and eighty-seven pupils arrived and—miraculously, it seemed—were all settled in their classes by 10 a.m.

An essential part of Charles Oxley's educational philosophy—and one which was soon to be under attack through Hamilton College— was his belief in corporal punishment being available to deal with bullies and vandals. 'Spare the rod and spoil the child' was not just a useful Bible text to justify corporal punishment; taken with the whole thrust of scriptural teaching, it was part of the way for parents and teachers to bring up children in a godly way. A Christian view of education would always want to encourage positive attitudes—to God, to adults, to one's peers, to the environment, to work—and so it must also discourage wrong attitudes. The question which Charles often asked and which nobody answered adequately, was: How do you punish thugs and bullies effectively if you do not have the sanction of corporal punishment?

His stance on this issue had brought him into many a wrangle with STOPP—the Society of Teachers opposed to Physical Punishment. (Charles always maintained that they were in fact *ex*-teachers who had formed a pressure group for political purposes. Their sponsors came mainly from the left-wing and liberal areas of public life, with the odd cleric thrown in.)

In his usual thorough manner, he had kept a careful check on STOPP's public utterances for many years and was never slow to attack them in newspaper correspondence columns. In the *Liverpool Daily Post* of 16th July 1982 he wrote:—

> I would like to ask Tom Scott of STOPP what punishments he would use in the following cases: 1. A 15-year-old boy is discovered to have been bullying an 11-year-old boy over a period of weeks, making the younger boy's life a misery and adversely affecting his education. 2. Three 12-year-old boys break into a school biology laboratory and torture and kill six hamsters. 3. Four 15-year-old boys ambush a 13-year-old boy learning the cello at school—they set upon him, smash his cello and stamp on his hand, breaking his fingers.

Scott's reply was that he 'would have to know a great deal more about the circumstances of each incident, but also about the children concerned, before I could even attempt to answer that question ... Teachers must take into account individual circumstances and personalities before deciding what to do.' At no point in his letter did he mention even a range of punishments from which he might perhaps select one that would be appropriate.

Charles swung back into the attack:—

> As I expected, Tom Scott failed to prescribe any alternative punishment to a good hiding for the thugs and bullies whose cases I quoted. This is the fatal flaw in the abolitionists' argument: they cannot come up with any adequate alternative. There were no special circumstances in the cases I quoted. But what possible 'individual circumstances and personalities', short of insanity, could possibly excuse or mitigate the deliberate killing of hamsters or the deliberate breaking of a boy's fingers to stop him playing the cello?

To Scott's claim that 'beating the culprit will only make matters worse', Charles replied, 'What rubbish! There are thousands of decent law-abiding citizens in Liverpool alone who will confirm that when heading for trouble as youngsters they were smartly brought back into line with the firm application of a cane or a slipper.'

In early March 1983 the *Liverpool Daily Post* published a letter from Paul Temperton of STOPP quoting statistics and extracts from a Home Office report and claiming that corporal punishment is not an effective deterrent. Charles recognised where these statistics came from and was quick to point out that they were out of date (1920 and 1938) and irrelevant (they related to birching criminal offenders, not caning schoolboys). He challenged Temperton as to why he closed his mind 'to the obvious fact that when children were disciplined at home with a slipper and at school with a cane and when violent thugs were birched and murderers hanged, there was much less crime and much less fear of burglary and violent assault?'

In November 1983 the *Times Educational Supplement* published a full-page feature on Charles Oxley in the wake of his exposure of the Paedophile Information Exchange. Entitled 'The Lord's Business', Bert Lodge's article presented a very fair summary of Charles' educational principles, offering, as Charles was the first to admit, 'a good balance between uncritical approval and overt rejection. Even I saw he had his tongue in his cheek at times.' Towards the end of the article, Lodge referred to the many campaigns in which Charles was involved—including those 'against sex shops, X films, STOPP ("They were using emotive language and bogus statistics. They're doing a terrible disservice to children.") ...'

Tom Scott wrote a letter of complaint to the *TES*, describing Bert Lodge's article as 'obsequious', objecting to what Charles had said about STOPP and challenging him to produce 'a shred of evidence to support his ludicrous claim.'

> I cannot deny we sometimes use 'emotive' language, but so of course do our opponents. No one with an ounce of sensitivity could work in this office for long without feeling outraged by the brutality meted out to children in schools throughout the country. I know who is 'doing a terrible disservice to children'.
>
> Finally, it does seem extraordinary to me that Oxley can campaign against both sex shops (he is vice-chairman of Mrs Whitehouse's NVALA) *and* STOPP. The fact is that the existence of child-beating in schools can lead to the development of sado-masochistic tendencies. And many pornographic magazines cater for those who are obsessed with the subject of beating.

Charles must have licked his lips when he read this challenge. In his reply, as well as reiterating the corrections he had addressed to Paul Temperton a few months earlier, he also wrote the following:—

STOPP selects one particular offence and claims that crime decreased after 1948, the year judicial corporal punishment was abolished. The true and broader story is that the number of crimes of violence (not including sexual assaults) jumped from 1,509 in 1947 to 82,257 in 1977 and to 97,200 in 1980.

STOPP claims support from the Cadogan Report of 1938 but they do not point out that this report refers to corporal punishments in Borstal institutions and has no relevance to comprehensive education in 1983.

STOPP's Research Co-ordinator wrote recently: 'Britain is already 200 years behind the times. Poland banned corporal punishment in 1783!' (*St Helens Reporter* 20.11.83) He did not tell us that Poland was not a nation at that time but divided among Prussia, Russia and Austria, that it did not have free compulsory education until 1921 and that in 1945 the involvement of the Church in education was severely restricted and non-Communist teachers lost their jobs and some lost their lives.

They set France as a shining example of civilised school punishments, but they do not point out the different legal position and educational philosophy of French education. I telephoned a French Consulate three years ago to ask what action would be taken against a 13-year-old boy who persistently bullied younger and smaller boys. The reply was, 'Ah, I used to be a teacher. One of the tougher teachers would ... how you say ... sort him out.' 'You mean, he would take him behind the cycle-shed and give him a good thumping?' I asked. 'Yes, exactly,' she replied.

Not only are their statistics and arguments bogus, the whole organisation is bogus. They call themselves a 'Society of Teachers ...', but they are not practising teachers. They are political campaigners lobbying MPs, pressurising the unions and badgering Local Education Authorities.

Tom Scott must be extraordinarily dim if he cannot understand why a person who is prepared to protect his pupils by whacking the bottoms of thieves and bullies, is also prepared to try to protect children by campaigning against pornographers and paedophiles.

It was just a year later, November 1984, when Tom Scott and Charles Oxley came face to face in—of all places—a Fleet Street pub. STOPP had called a press conference at this venue to publicise a dossier of alleged beatings of schoolchildren. Their letter to the Education Secretary of the day, Sir Keith Joseph, deplored 'some teachers who have callously taken advantage of children entrusted to their care' and believed Sir Keith would be 'appalled by ... incidents which show that some beatings are just crude sexual assaults by sadistic teachers.'

The report of the press conference in the following day's *Daily Telegraph* highlighted not so much the claims of STOPP as the confrontation between their campaign organiser and his arch-enemy, Charles Oxley. 'TAKE NO NOTICE OF STOPP'S "SEX BEATINGS" CLAIM SAYS HEADMASTER' proclaimed the headline over a four-column report.

Charles' presence at the press conference was not just for ideological reasons but because Hamilton College was one of the schools named in the STOPP dossier. A six-year-old boy had been admitted to the College without his parents revealing that he had a history of disruptive behaviour and was undergoing psychiatric treatment. From his first day at Hamilton he was scribbling on other children's work, breaking their toys, squeezing them round the neck or giving them bear hugs. Reprimands from the class teacher soon led to smacks on his trousered bottom with the palm of the teacher's hand, then on the palm of his hand with the flat side of a ruler. All to no avail. Letters home brought no response, so when the boy in his fifth week at Hamilton College wrenched a toilet door off its hinges, Charles told the parents he must leave. When the parents came to see him he advised them to seek the help of a psychiatrist, whereupon they admitted that he was already having psychiatric help. The father complained that Charles had not himself punished the child. The mother contacted the local press complaining that Charles had been unable to control a six-year-old boy.

A report of all this reached Tom Scott, who wrote to Hamilton College under a false name, T South, from London. He stated that he was moving to Scotland and wanted his children—Avril, aged 12, and John, aged 5—admitted to Hamilton College. In his letter he wrote, 'I trust that the belt is used regularly by all teachers on both boys and girls. If this is not the case, I may have to consider another school.' He sent three letters in all and in reference to the case of the six-year-old boy said, 'Several good thrashings would surely have brought him to his senses.' Charles' suspicions had been aroused by this correspondence and, finding the number through directory enquiries, he telephoned 'T South' and found himself talking to none other than Tom Scott.

Charles had received a tip-off that Hamilton College was named in STOPP's booklet, 'Catalogue of Cruelty', so he quickly ran off copies of the 'T South' correspondence and hastened to London in time for the Fleet Street press conference. There, he distributed the evidence of Scott's deception and challenged the validity of the STOPP booklet's claims. Scott tried to justify his action by saying that Charles had used a pseudonym to infiltrate the Paedophile Information Exchange.

'But I was investigating criminal offences,' said Charles; 'he was not. I did not express agreement with what I opposed nor did I boast of practising it; Mr Scott did both. I obtained information which was otherwise unobtainable; the information Mr Scott obtained was available to all parents. Apart from using a pseudonym I told no lies; Mr Scott's three letters were full of lies, for he has no children and was not moving to Scotland. I did not act as an agent provocateur; he did. I was careful to get my facts right and to present a true report to New Scotland Yard; Mr Scott did not get his facts right and has presented a false and inaccurate report to the Press and to Sir Keith Joseph.'

There were to be more rumblings of discontent in the House of Commons about the sale of the college buildings and the running of the school. In March 1986, the Labour MP for Carrick, Cumnock and Doon Valley, George Foulkes, in a debate about Scottish Tertiary Education, lamented what he called 'the scandal of the sale of the Hamilton College buildings at a knockdown price. They were sold to a somewhat dubious character who is also involved in a pretty sinister campaign for law and order. To sell Hamilton College to a sort of Mary Whitehouse in trousers is not a sensible step. I hope that the Minister will get his inspectors to look at what is going on in that private institution. It would bear very careful scrutiny.'

What Mr Foulkes did not know, until Charles quickly put him right, was that eighteen members of Her Majesty's Inspectorate of Schools had just completed a six-week investigation of the school, as a result of which full registration was granted to Hamilton College by the Scottish Education Department two weeks before Mr Foulkes made his ill-judged remarks.

Charles' understandable anger led him to write to the MP demanding that he either substantiate what he had said or withdraw his remarks. Foulkes' terse reply stated: 'I have nothing to add to my comments in the House.' Charles followed up with this: 'I challenge you to repeat publicly the untrue and offensive remarks which you made about me and my school in the House of Commons while hiding under parliamentary privilege.' He received no further reply, and even a letter to the Speaker of the House, though receiving a sympathetic reply, could not force Foulkes either to substantiate or to withdraw what he had said.

One interesting and perhaps surprising element in the early growth of Hamilton College was the number of children from Asian backgrounds, many of them Muslims, who were enrolled. They maintained a steady twenty percent of the school population, even though their parents knew their children would attend a Bible-based Christian morning assembly and two lessons per week of Bible-based Religious Education. The only concessions made to their background were in respect of diet and in allowing the older girls to wear long stockings.

At a parents' evening a Muslim father said to Charles, 'I thank God every day that you started the school here.' Charles found that Hindu and Muslim parents wanted to send their children to his school partly because the pupils are expected to work hard to achieve academic success and partly because they knew their children, especially the girls, would not be exposed to vulgarity.

Some Islamic leaders in the community, however, were not happy about Muslim children attending Hamilton College and wrote to ask for concessions, including the provision of Islamic teaching as an alternative to Christian R.E. Charles was in a strong position to be able to give a polite refusal to such requests, particularly as the prospectuses of all his schools stated clearly the Christian ethos and teaching that parents could expect for their children.

Although the College building has four floors, only the ground floor and a few rooms on the first floor were needed when the school opened. The local council said he would not have to pay rates on the other two floors as long as they were unoccupied and available for let. The Hamilton District Council would not allow the third and fourth storeys to be used for anything other than educational purposes, but in spite of advertising over a long period, nobody came forward to use the upper floors. The staunch Labour council was reluctant to grant rates relief to the educational entrepreneur from England and it was not until September 1986, when the school had been operating for three years, that the finance committee finally agreed to rates relief of £98,000 for the period between January 1984 and March 1986. The school had already paid £46,000, which was held in credit for future payments. As the chairman of the finance committee observed, 'Our feelings about the owners of the school are immaterial. What is important is that they have met our criteria. If we were to refuse the appeal our action would not stand up in the courts.'

Charles did fall foul of the authorities in April 1986 when he found himself up before the Equal Opportunities Commission. Back in September 1985, one of his Junior School teachers had left with hardly any notice, affecting not only her class but also the four children she brought in her car from the Edinburgh area each day. Charles advertised in *The Scotsman*, an Edinburgh-based newspaper, for a replacement to start as soon as possible. Among the fifteen applications came one from a Mrs Robbins, who lived in Callander, a town further away and less easily accessible from Hamilton.

Mrs Robbins' geographical situation was not the only reason to question her suitability for the post: her training and experience were not in the age group specified in the advertisement; her salary was considerably higher than she could expect at Hamilton; her spelling and handwriting fell some way short of Charles' normal expectations; and another lady applicant fulfilled the requirements of the post much more acceptably.

In his letter to Mrs Robbins, however, Charles did not mention any of these factors but unfortunately wrote the following sentence: 'I regret I cannot proceed with your application because our policy is not to appoint lady teachers with very young children.' In her application, Mrs Robbins had given the ages of her children as fourteen, five, three and two, so Charles felt that her prime concern must always and rightly be her own offspring rather than the pupils of Hamilton College. If one of her children were to be sick in the night, he would not expect Mrs Robbins to be in school the next day. He would therefore rather appoint someone with less constricting family commitments.

Mrs Robbins did not reply to Charles' letter. The next he knew about the matter was three months later when he received an order to appear before an industrial tribunal to answer a charge under the Sex Discrimination Act 1975.

What emerged from the hearing was that there was no actual policy in Charles' schools not to appoint women on the grounds of having very young children. Teachers came into that category who taught at Tower College and Scarisbrick Hall as well as Hamilton College. Yet, because that was the only reason given for Charles' refusal of Mrs Robbins' application for employment, she won her case. The tribunal made a 'token award' of £100 as 'compensation for injury to feelings.'

Charles had learnt his lesson—to be more careful in the wording of letters in such delicate areas—but he was unrepentant. He could have avoided any adverse publicity by agreeing to an out-of-court settlement before the hearing, as his solicitor advised him to do, but he felt there was a valid point to be made. In a press statement after the case he said: 'It is natural and normal to assume that mothers, rather than fathers, will take responsibility for very young children, but the Sex Discrimination Act does not think so. A woman with four children aged fourteen, five, three and two and a husband in full-time employment cannot be expected to do a full-time teaching job as well.' So much for the tentacles of political correctness which were beginning to reach across the Atlantic by the mid-eighties.

§

DURING THE TIME when Charles and Muriel were setting up their new school at Hamilton, their cars must almost have worn their own individual ruts on the M6 and A74 from Lancashire to the south-east fringes of Glasgow. Charles reckoned that the 205-mile journey from Tower took him three hours, usually including a stop for coffee and a stretch of those long legs at Gretna. Hamilton College had a warden's flat which he used for overnight stops, so, during the first two years of directing affairs at Hamilton, he would drive up on Monday morning to be at the College for 9.00 a.m., stay there Monday night and return home on Tuesday evening. Wednesday he would spend with Tower, Scarisbrick and anything else. Then he would be up and away early on Thursday to put in two more full days at Hamilton, normally travelling south late on Friday night, unless there happened to be a parents' showround or an entrance examination on Saturday morning.

Driving more than eight hundred miles per week over a total of about twelve hours would tempt anyone to exceed the speed limit on occasions, and Charles made the acquaintance of the police forces of Lancashire, Cumbria and Scotland. He never made a fuss about losing his driving licence, but it became evident that he was either being driven around by the long-suffering Muriel or he was making use of British Rail. This turned out to be something of a blessing in disguise, because either of these alternatives gave him the chance to do some work en route and even—dare one suggest it?—relax!

In fact, he may have become a little too relaxed on one of his rail journeys north, because, when he alighted from the Liverpool-Glasgow train at Motherwell station, he realised he had left on the luggage rack a leather holdall containing wage packets for cleaners and domestic staff at Hamilton College. He turned and ran back along the platform, but the train was already pulling out. Reporting the matter to the station-master, he was assured after a couple of telephone calls that a porter would collect the bag when the train arrived at Glasgow Central.

An hour later, the Glasgow lost property office reported that the holdall had been found and the wage packets were still in it. Charles was mightily relieved, but not for long.

'Can you tell me how much money there is in the packets?' asked the railway official over the phone.

'Sorry, I've no idea,' replied Charles. Wage rates for cleaners were Muriel's domain, not his.

'In that case, we'll have to open each of the packets and count the cash.'

'You can't do that!' protested Charles. 'Only the people who are due to get those wages should be able to do that.'

'Sorry, sir, but British Rail procedure is that we have to open all the packets and count the money, and then it will be handed back to you on payment of £40.'

Charles was furious. He rushed to the station and found the lost property office. Sure enough, every wage packet had been slit open and, despite his protests, he had to write out a cheque for £40 before he could take the money away.

As so often, he transferred his sense of injustice to the typewriter. He wrote directly to the Chairman of British Rail with a full account of the incident and claimed that the maximum charge of £40 for the recovery of money was most unfair. If an old lady, in the confusion of alighting from a busy train, left her handbag with £400 of her life savings, she too would have to pay £40 for its recovery and return. The reply Charles received, explaining British Rail's policy, contained a refund of £20. Although grateful, he was not satisfied; the policy needed to be changed.

He wrote to the Under Secretary for Railways in London. He wrote to the Central Transport Consultative Committee. He wrote to his solicitor. He wrote to the *Sunday Express*, who made a news item out of it. He even wrote to Jimmy Savile, then a television favourite with the programme *Jim'll Fix It*, explaining BR's policy and concluding: 'I hope you agree with me that a fixed penalty of say £5, which could be reduced or waived at the discretion of an official, would be more appropriate and fair. Do you think you could fix it?'

Of all these potential allies in this cause it was the Central Transport Consultative Committee that took up the matter with British Rail. First indications were that there would be no alteration in their policy, but in the end the maximum charge was reduced from £40 to £5, much to Charles' delight.

'My seven-month battle has resulted in a better deal for railway passengers ... at least for the forgetful ones!' He did not begrudge the time, the typing or the expense of winning that battle, even though the solicitor's investigations into the legality of BR bye-laws cost him £57!

A rather different experience with a British Rail inspector had him chuckling to himself like a schoolboy. Sixty-one-year-old Charles Oxley had his ticket punched by the inspector, who said, 'Thank-you, son,' as he handed it back.

Chapter 12

DISMAY AT DECLINING STANDARDS

During the later years of his life, Charles Oxley believed that his personal battle for Britain was being lost. Not that he gave up the fight, because, like the army's standard-bearer on the battlefields of old, he would still stand bravely when other warriors fell or turned tail. He was, however, realist enough to recognise that the waves of secular liberal humanism were gradually eroding the brittle cliffs of Christian morality. What particularly grieved him was the lack of resistance among church leaders, some of whom stood unashamedly among the non-Christian ranks. He looked back to the first generation of Christians who challenged both the sophistry of Greek philosophers and the sadistic cruelty of Roman emperors and came through victorious, even in death. It was Christianity that had offered the means of saving civilisation when the Roman Empire crumbled; it was Christianity that had sustained intellectual life through the Middle Ages.

The permissive society of the contemporary Western world is a more subtle battle ground [he wrote], and, for the most part, professing Christians have failed to engage the enemy. Consequently, the battle is all but lost. The shameful failure of the Church to defend and proclaim the Gospel has permitted and facilitated the alarming success of humanists to spread atheism and atheistic attitudes throughout the land, especially among young people.

An infuriating feature of this struggle is the high proportion of senior and middle-ranking officers of Christ's army, who hold their commission but are in fact fighting on the enemy's side. The rank and file are consequently confused and, without effective leadership, have drifted away from the battle field.

He regarded the permissive society as essentially a God-defying society and had no doubt that the collapse of the moral structure resulted from the downgrading of the Scriptures. From being generally accepted as the inspired Word of God, the Bible had come to be regarded as just a collection of writings on a par with books from other religions; it held interest for academics and theologians, but not the compelling message or particular relevance for modern western culture. Charles felt that the biblical doctrine of mankind, as set out in Genesis and Paul's Letter to the Romans, had been usurped by man-centred philosophies of Charles Darwin, Sigmund Freud, John Stuart Mill and Karl Marx.

Charles further noted the emergence of various synthetic 'gospels' in which any reference to judgement or damnation was removed and the whole emphasis was on a God of love who would accept everyone and tolerate virtually anything. Gone was the need to repent from personal sinfulness in order to receive forgiveness and salvation; gone were the dangers of spending eternity in hell, separated from a holy God by one's refusal to acknowledge Jesus as Lord and Saviour. 'Tolerance is today's cardinal virtue,' he wrote, 'and many professing Christians have become more compassionate than Christ himself.'

He had no time for the British Council of Churches or the World Council of Churches, both of whom he regarded as traitors to the cause of the Kingdom of God. Both groupings appeared to equate the Christian gospel with socialism, if not Marxism. Pauline Webb, a tireless spokeswoman for both bodies in the 1970s, told a group called 'Liberation' in 1977: 'The Christian faith is an agent of world revolution and the purpose of the ecumenical movement is not ... to unite Christians, but to unite all mankind under a world socialist state.'

Charles read with anger and dismay the words of the South Bank theologians of the 1960s, trying to make Christ 'relevant' by propounding the so-called 'new morality'. (Charles was not alone in thinking this phenomenon bore a striking resemblance to the old immorality!) Dr John Robinson, Bishop of Woolwich, claimed, 'There are no unbreakable rules ... because, as it were, it (love) has a built-in moral compass, enabling it to home intuitively upon the deepest needs of the other, and can allow itself to be directed completely by the situation.' Thus was born 'situation ethics', a challenge to the unchangeable law of God and denying all moral absolutes. These and other theologians, believing that twentieth-century man with his increasing scientific knowledge and technological advance would not acknowledge anything of the supernatural in the life and work of Jesus Christ, sought to 'demythologise' the Gospel by removing anything miraculous, including the virgin birth and the resurrection of Jesus. Man had, after all, come of age and did not need 'a god out there'; Jesus was 'a man for others' and the Gospel was a matter of following his example in showing love to others.

Staunch opponents of Christianity gleefully picked up on these philosophies which emphasised the humanity of Jesus at the expense of his divinity and replaced the supernatural with the secular. Barbara Smoker, of the National Secular Society, in an article 'The Faith all at Sea', published in the *Freethinker* in October 1984, referred particularly to Don Cupitt, Dean of Emmanuel College, Cambridge, and David Jenkins, Bishop of Durham, when she wrote perceptively that '... for some decades now there has been a far greater ideological gulf between the modern theologian and the average pious Christian than between the modern theologian and any atheist ... *The theologians are doing our job for us these days—and doing it better than we would be allowed the resources to do.*' (italics added)

It was also Dr John Robinson who described the permissive society as 'a step towards maturity' and voluntarily entered the witness box to defend the publication of *Lady Chatterley's Lover* when it was challenged under the 1959 Obscene Publications Act. He referred to the immoral sexual relationship described in the book as being 'in a real sense something sacred, an act of Holy Communion.' Charles' comment was that Robinson 'could not possibly have defended that book had he not already relinquished his hold on Biblical truth.'

In other areas too Charles saw the churches retreating from the front line of the battle for Christian standards. The day before the Commons debated the restoration of the death penalty on July 13th 1983, the General Synod of the Church of England debated the motion 'that this Synod would deplore the reintroduction of capital punishment ...' They voted 407 to 36 for this motion, ignoring No. 37 of the Thirty-Nine Articles, which specifically acknowledges the right and duty of the civil power in this matter. The Archbishop of Canterbury said, 'I do not believe in a God of judgment.' He described capital punishment as 'barbaric'. The Roman Catholic bishops of England, Wales and Northern Ireland appealed to Parliament not to restore capital punishment. The Roman Catholic Bishop of Londonderry, Mgr Edward Daly, warned of 'dreadful consequences if the death penalty were reintroduced'.

Charles protested vigorously at such remarks. 'This is blackmail! The terrorists are able to dictate to us that if we try to stop them murdering people by restoring the death penalty, they will commit more murders. Justice is in full retreat.'

The Methodist Church also declared its opposition to capital punishment. The United Reformed Church gave its support to the British Council of Churches' attitude and voted against reintroduction. They gave as their first reason 'Christian reverence and respect for all human life as God's gift'. They could not see that it is precisely because of the sacredness of human life that the only penalty which demonstrates the seriousness of the crime is the forfeiture of the murderer's own life.

At the time of the 1983 debate on the restoration of capital punishment, the *Liverpool Daily Post* published the following letter from Charles Oxley:—

Thank you for giving front-page prominence to the Archbishop of Canterbury's description of hanging as a 'barbarous punishment' (7th July).

Terrorist bombings and brutal murders are also barbaric and we must face the question, how does a civilised society adequately punish acts of barbarism?

There is a widespread and deeply felt conviction that the present indeterminate prison sentence is inadequate and unfair and that the death penalty is the only appropriate punishment.

Many advocates of capital punishment, including myself, would favour a different method of execution. But the Archbishop was referring to execution by any means.

One would have expected an archbishop to base his belief on the Bible and the centuries-old teaching of the Christian Church on this issue. How can a Church leader reject the teaching of Genesis 9:6, Exodus 21:12, Leviticus 24:17, Numbers 35:14-16, Deuteronomy 19:11 and other passages too numerous to mention?

You report that Dr Runcie said capital punishment would give the state powers that were 'too God-like', but in Romans 13 the State is described as 'the powers that be ordained of God' to act as the agent and minister of God and as 'an avenger for wrath to him that doeth evil', a duty acknowledged by Jesus (John 9:11), St Peter (1 Peter 2:14) and St Paul (Acts 25:11).

It is the Archbishop who is being 'God-like' in setting his own views above those of God Himself. He is trying to be more Christian than Christ.

The death penalty lies at the very foundation of the Gospel, for 'without the shedding of blood there is no remission of sin' (Hebrews 9:22). Abolish the death penalty and you make the death of Christ an unfortunate tragedy rather than the voluntary acceptance of God's judgement on sin.

The death penalty is Biblical and Christian and it is our present violent, lawless, Godless society that is barbaric. Indeed, it is worse than barbaric, for we are not emerging from barbarism into civilisation, but deliberately rejecting Christian standards and sliding into self-destroying anarchy.

It is significant that the move away from *capital* punishment by some churchmen has coincided with their abandonment of belief in *eternal* punishment in hell and the need for personal salvation by repentance and faith in Christ. The teaching of the uncompromising Christ has been misinterpreted into a mushy humanism.

Those who do not base their beliefs on the Bible should at least listen to those at the sharp end of our violent society—elderly city-dwellers, the police and prison officers not compromising clerics in cloistered cathedrals.

Although the leaders of the major denominations opposed the restoration of the death penalty, Charles did find some men of God who followed the biblical line. Rev. Eddy Stride, who worked in the

East End of London, courageously condemned the Church of England Synod for its unbiblical stance. He stressed that there was a difference between the murdered victim's relatives seeking *revenge* and the State's duty to *avenge*. Rev. John Stott, a leading evangelical and Rector of All Souls, Langham Place, clearly explained the true biblical demand for the death penalty when he spoke on Radio 4's *Sunday* programme and in a series of articles in the *Christian Weekly News*.

In the area of sexual ethics also Church leaders fell short of clear, uncompromising statements. As the dreadful spectre of AIDS began to cast its shadow over the nation and the world, principally through homosexual behaviour, the two highest ranking churchmen in the Church of England failed to condemn homosexual practices. The Archbishop of Canterbury described homosexuality as a 'handicap' and the Archbishop of York, Dr Habgood, referred to it as a 'misfortune'. It took a Christian Chief Constable, James Anderton, of the Greater Manchester police, to declare in plain language that 'Sodomy is sinful', a remark which provoked some very nasty criticism from many quarters.

Charles regretted the failure of the churches to stamp out heresy and immorality within their own ranks. It seemed clear to him that the majority of professing Christians were largely unaware of what was taking place. 'Who could have imagined forty years ago that there would be a clergy-led Buggery Acceptance Campaign, euphemistically called the "Gay Christian Movement"?' he wrote. 'Instead of a mighty roar of protest at the attacks on our Christian faith and morals, there were a few 'tut-tuts' and some ineffective wringing of hands.'

He himself continued to utter many a roar of protest at any sign of further decline in moral standards. When Priscilla Presley was considering whether to accept £70,000 to have her baby's birth filmed and shown in an episode of *Dallas*, he at once gave his views to the *Liverpool Echo*. Under the headline 'Oxley Fury Over Screen Baby', his words put the incident into perspective: 'The whole thing is indecent. She is not married and is being offered money to parade her child's illegitimacy in front of millions. That is glorying in sin and utterly shameless. Only 50 years ago people would be ashamed to produce a child out of wedlock. This case shows just how far standards have slipped in Western society. I feel terribly sorry for the child. There are some people in show business who are decent but the majority seem to have problems in upholding reasonable standards of behaviour.'

A rumour that reached Charles' ears seemed to suggest that the BBC had really ditched its original standards. Having been told that a famous inscription in the foyer of Broadcasting House had been either removed or replaced, he wrote to ask if it was true. It was not. The Latin inscription had remained unchanged from 1932, the year in which Broadcasting House became fully operational; in the process of redecorating in 1985 the English translation was being moved from the wall to a glass cabinet. One wonders whether the words should be engraved on the office wall of every producer and programme controller in the BBC:—

THIS TEMPLE OF THE ARTS AND MUSES IS DEDICATED TO ALMIGHTY GOD BY THE FIRST GOVERNORS OF BROADCASTING IN THE YEAR 1931, SIR JOHN REITH BEING THE DIRECTOR GENERAL. IT IS THEIR PRAYER THAT GOOD SEED SOWN MAY BRING FORTH A GOOD HARVEST AND THAT THE PEOPLE, INCLINING THEIR EAR TO WHATSOEVER THINGS ARE BEAUTIFUL AND HONEST AND OF GOOD REPORT, MAY TREAD THE PATH OF WISDOM AND UPRIGHTNESS.

Charles deliberately stayed away from the political arena himself, although he had friends and supporters from across the party spectrum. More than one person suggested he should stand for Parliament, but he could never have been a battery-hen party-liner; he needed a free-range environment in order to be able to highlight what he saw as the nation's ills. A correspondent in the *St Helens Reporter* once labelled him 'a right-wing extremist' because of his views on law and order. Charles wrote to reply: 'I am not associated in any way with any political party and never have been. I have publicly denounced the National Front's line on race and immigration.' On the other hand, he also publicly denounced the firemen when they took strike action in support of a pay claim, his own years in the fire service earning him the right to comment. At the same time he blamed successive governments for giving in to trade union power. He pointed to the lifeboatmen as supreme examples of unselfish sacrificial service in a generally greedy society.

Somebody somewhere must have thought he should be a member of the Conservative Party, because one day in 1984 he received a letter from the party chairman, John Selwyn Gummer, offering membership and inviting his comments on any issues of current concern to him. Such an opportunity was too good to miss.

I have not joined the Party (a) because I believe the nation's problem is basically a spiritual one and I have used my time and energies in trying to advance the cause of evangelical Christianity, and (b) I have been very disappointed with previous Conservative Governments and am very disappointed with the present Government.

I regard nearly all present Government ministers as a bunch of wet nellies. As a schoolmaster who thinks in terms of PASS and FAIL, I must write FAIL as the final assessment.

1   Failure to restore capital punishment for murder.
2   Failure to deal with rising incidence of violent crime, armed robbery and rape.
3   Failure to deal with terrorism and with the IRA in particular.
4   Failure to deal with hooliganism and vandalism.
5   Failure to deal with pornography and the proliferation of sex establishments.
6   Failure to deal with the national scandal of abortion.
7   Failure to ensure that the 1944 Education Act provisions for religious instruction are observed.

The list actually extended to sixteen 'failures'. Charles was not surprised that his letter did not receive a reply.

His political evenhandedness can be seen in his reaction to a four-page paper distributed free of charge by the Labour-led Merseyside County Council: 'I am writing to object to political propaganda sent out in this way. Reading the paper makes me more than ever convinced that the decision to abolish the Metropolitan County Councils is a good one and should be implemented without delay.' Merseyside as a region was close to Charles' heart, not only because he lived there, but also because he was Chairman of the Merseyside Community Standards Association, in which he mobilised a faithful group of good-hearted citizens, led by Mr and Mrs Raymond Taylor.

In the run-up to the 1983 General Election, someone had written to the *Liverpool Daily Post* expressing the hope that the Social Democratic Party (in the days of the 'Gang of Four') would be able to restore law and order. Charles replied with a catalogue of legislation introduced when Roy Jenkins was Home Secretary in a Labour

Government. The Obscene Publications Act had opened the door via Lady Chatterley to floods of pornography; capital and corporal punishment had been abolished; the Abortion Law had led to the killing of two million babies before birth; the removal of theatre censorship had allowed gross obscenity onto the public stage; divorce had been made easier to obtain; parole rules had been eased and even murderers could obtain bail.

> No political party, not even Parliament itself, has any hope now of restoring law and order, because the majority of MP's have changed the basis of our laws and apply misguided political expediency rather than solid Christian principles.

When Sunday trading came up for public debate in 1985, Charles voiced an interesting suggestion in an interview on BBC Radio Merseyside: 'If all the shops are going to open on Sundays, then Christians ought to protest by ringing all the church bells on Saturdays between 6 a.m. and 6 p.m.'

He himself had no qualms of conscience about working on Sundays as the principal of a boarding school, and he recognised that a proportion of the workforce in essential jobs had to work on a Sunday. At the same time he wanted the nation generally to respect the Lord's Day, even if they turned their backs on the Lord himself. When he received an invitation from the Bishop of Warrington to an Industry Year North-West Conference chaired by Brian Redhead of the BBC, he was horrified to find it was scheduled for a Sunday between 10 a.m. and 4 p.m., with Church representatives heavily involved. He sent a brief reply expressing his surprise that it was to be held on a Sunday and saying that 'it is for this reason that I am unable to attend.'

Charles saw declining standards in public life being matched by a deterioration also in educational standards. In 1975 he had spoken out against the new system of giving GCE Ordinary Level certificates to candidates with grade D or E, which were below the pass level. The whole concept of 'Pass' and 'Fail' was disappearing and Charles deplored this deliberate lowering of standards as a ploy of egalitarian social engineering. He wrote immediately to the GCE examining boards and to the press, suggesting that the move had occurred as a deliberate policy to disguise the failures of the comprehensive system of education.

Ten years later the amalgamation of GCE Ordinary Level with CSE to make the new General Certificate of Secondary Education (GCSE) brought further strong disapproval. 'It puts control of the syllabuses and even teaching methods firmly into the hands of central government and shifts the emphasis away from academic and cultural studies to practical skills designed to train young people for industrial employment,' wrote Charles in a newsletter to Tower College parents.

He was certainly not alone in feeling concern about the new examination. *The Mail on Sunday* asked Charles if they could investigate the standards of the proposed exam by giving a mathematics paper to some Tower College pupils. State comprehensives had refused to co-operate, but Charles readily made his pupils available to take the test under examination conditions. However, a paper designed to be taken by 16-year-olds was given to Tower children of 11 and 12 at the beginning of September 1986. Of the twenty-eight children—nearly all of whom had been at Tower from the age of four and were therefore not 'selected' in the normal sense—all passed Paper One with an average of 75% and twenty-five of them passed Paper Two with an average of 52%. The children themselves thought it must be some kind of trick as they found it all so easy. 'It was simple arithmetic that we are taught in junior school,' said one boy, who was disappointed to have scored only 99%.

The following Sunday, the Opinion column in *The Mail on Sunday* began: 'Rarely has this newspaper received such a response to an article as our investigation last week into the new GCSE exam.' The column mentioned attempts by the Department of Education and by the Education Secretary, Kenneth Baker, to play down the furore roused by the test, but the response of parents had reinforced general concern that standards expected of sixteen-year-olds would be much too low.

The change to GCSE required new textbooks in almost every subject. When *English: An Integrated Course* arrived on Charles' desk, a first quick glance aroused suspicions which led to a thorough perusal of the contents. Eventually he wrote to the publishers, to the Secretary of State for Education and to the *Liverpool Echo*, which featured Charles' concern on its front page. He took exception to many of the extracts selected in the book for study by young teenagers, because they contained blasphemies, vulgarity of language and attitudes which undermined the moral standards he had always fought to maintain.

The publishers threatened him with a libel action but never proceeded, and Kenneth Baker refused to take this action which Charles suggested: 'I respectfully request that you issue a statement urging parents to look at the books and resource material issued to their children and to protest to the headteacher if they think anything issued is morally harmful.'

This was not the first time Charles had taken a stand against the use of unsuitable literature in schools. In 1982 an elder in a Brethren assembly in Southport sought Charles' advice as to how to lodge a protest about the bad language and indecency in his daughter's class reader, *The Machine Gunners*.

Then in September 1983, just as Hamilton College was embarking on its first term, a man in Motherwell contacted Charles to ask for moral support; he was being prosecuted for keeping his two teenage daughters off school. They had been issued with a reading book which he considered quite unsuitable and possibly obscene. Despite the huge demands on his time from the new school, Charles actually went to the court and gave evidence on the man's behalf. Although the Sheriff accepted that the objection was 'sincere and genuine', he ruled that the man did not have reasonable cause for withdrawing his children from school. However, no penalty was imposed and the man had to pay only £6.50 costs. The case achieved some publicity in the Scottish press, aided by Charles' assertion that it should not have been the girls' father who was in the dock but those who allowed corrupting literature into the hands of impressionable schoolchildren.

GCSE Religious Studies also roused Charles' anger. Having checked all the syllabuses of all the Examination Boards he came to the conclusion that

> ... the GCSE Religious Studies syllabus is incompatible with the aims of a Christian school ... Christianity is seen as but one of several world religions, each of equal validity. Religion is seen as a human phenomenon and if pupils are made aware of the rites and customs of a few religions, it will promote good race relations through tolerance, today's virtue.

The pupils are encouraged to evaluate the minute amount of Biblical material prescribed, sixteen chapters of Mark's Gospel in one Board. But the Gospels were not written for the critical appraisal of 16-year-olds, but to show them the way, the truth and the life.

Right up to the end of his life Charles retained the hope that the independent schools would set up an independent examination board on the lines of the old GCE Ordinary Level to offer 'a traditional examination in traditional subjects, one which will be acceptable to universities and employers.' Six months before he died he read in the *Times Educational Supplement* of moves to reinstate the GCE 'O' Level and wrote a brief encouraging letter: 'Please regard me as an active supporter in this campaign and if GCE "O" Level is restored I will reintroduce it, entering about 80 candidates each year in academic subjects.' It seemed to him quite wrong that schools which chose to be independent of the state system of teaching could not also be independent of the examination system.

§

As a respected member of the Brethren movement, Charles had for years been concerned that many evangelical churches, especially among the Brethren, seemed reluctant to face up to issues in the world around them, preferring to maintain a strong line on Bible teaching without really applying biblical principles to contemporary problems. As a convener of the annual Conference of Brethren at Swanwick in Derbyshire, he was putting forward radical suggestions as far back as 1977 to alter the style and content of the conference. He recommended that a range of issues in contemporary society be addressed from a biblical perspective by experts in the field. That would have required inviting non-Brethren Christians to address the conference on some matters, but evidently the more conservative conveners could not go along with that idea, as 'Brethren truth' might be compromised.

History shows that evangelical Christians led the way in achieving social change in prison reform, the Factory Acts and abolition of the slave trade. Twentieth-century evangelicals were less prominent on social issues because they took the line that evangelism and deeper understanding of the scriptures were more important than being involved in politics or any other such 'worldly' activities. Charles disagreed. The Church needed to be 'active agents arresting the putrefaction in the world. In addition to our duty to proclaim the Gospel of God's offer of salvation, we have a responsibility to speak out boldly against wickedness, to refute error and to denounce hypocrisy, as did the Lord Himself.'

By the time of the 1984 Conference of Brethren, Charles had succeeded in at least having the speakers address some of the contemporary issues on which he felt the young in particular needed guidance. He himself was invited to speak on 'Decline into Darkness' under the overall heading of 'Light in the Dark—The Church and the World', with such men as the biblical scholar Professor FF Bruce and the MP Dr Brian Mawhinney sharing the platform.

The Brethren have had to face some harsh realities in the last quarter of the twentieth century: some of their most gifted men have moved to other streams of the Christian Church and attendance at the long-established weekly meetings declined noticeably in many assemblies. The content and style of those meetings needed to be held up to the light, as did the effectiveness of elders, the role of women, the 'threat' of the charismatic renewal movement and the ultra-conservative attitudes which produced a ghetto mentality among Brethren.

Although Charles and his forefathers were Brethren men to the core, he never assumed that all wisdom was to be found among the Brethren, but was happy to talk and listen to Christians from other traditions if they had worthwhile insights to offer. He would certainly never compromise biblical truth and he placed knowledge of the Scriptures very high on his list of priorities for any Christian. Where he differed from some of his fellow Brethren was in his readiness to examine exactly how biblical principles could be applied to moral and ethical issues. To argue a case from a biblical standpoint, especially with those who did not share his belief in the supreme authority of the Bible in matters of faith and conduct, required more than just quoting scriptures. He was ready to read and think and question in order to build a bridge of moral understanding from the Bible into a knotty problem.

Charles' determination to protect children from harmful influences was once again to the fore in 1986, when the mother of an eleven-year-old boy sought his help. The family lived on Humberside and the local Church of England vicar had allegedly committed sexual offences against the boy, but the police were unwilling to prosecute. Charles offered to bring a private prosecution if statements were obtained from at least two other children who were thought to have been molested. Only when Geoffrey Dickens raised the matter in the House of Commons were other mothers willing to come forward on behalf of their sons. It turned out that the vicar came from Sweden, was not properly qualified as a clergyman and owned a video shop in Hull which sold and hired out video 'nasties' and 'blue' films. Despite the widespread publicity that surrounded the case and a request from the Archbishop of York for the vicar to resign, the man continued to take services in his parish church. Charles therefore continued with the case, because under ecclesiastical law the Church of England could not take further action until criminal charges were brought.

In the end the arrested vicar died from a heart attack in his cell before the case could reach court. This episode illustrated how determined Charles Oxley was in seeking to root out wickedness as well as promote wholesome values in society. He felt it was well worth the considerable personal cost in time and money to see good triumph over evil.

Chapter 13

FINAL BATTLES

Although he had played the major role in smashing the Paedophile Information Exchange, Charles was fully aware that other individuals and groups were actively practising and promoting sex with children. He knew, for example, that paedophile propaganda was disseminated by the Lesbian and Gay Youth Movement, some of whose literature came into his hands in 1986. The LGYM, based in London, advertised summer camps, free of charge, for children under sixteen: 'Get away from parents, teachers and straights' was the offer; 'we are starting a lesbian and gay village under canvas.'

Charles discovered that such a camp was being held in Barnstaple, North Devon. He first contacted New Scotland Yard, who were very concerned but were unable to trace the people responsible because they used a private box number for replies to their adverts. Charles then contacted the Chief Constable of Devon and was put in touch with a very helpful Inspector, who made intensive enquiries but was unable to locate the camp. North Devon has literally hundreds of campsites busy in the month of August and the police could hardly be expected to check them all.

Charles' next strategy was to alert the press to what LGYM was doing. Together with Geoffrey Dickens MP, a redoubtable ally in such matters, he spoke out against the evil and sinister intentions of those who wanted to take other people's children away on holiday specifically to encourage homosexual behaviour. He had two aims in making the matter public: firstly, he hoped that the people of North Devon might themselves be able to locate the camp and report it to the police; secondly, he wanted to challenge the arrogance of the homosexual lobby which sought to present homosexuality as normal and acceptable.

The publicity earned him less than honourable mention in the next issue of the Lesbian and Gay Youth Movement's magazine. Scotland Yard then asked if he could discover the names and addresses of the Movement's leaders. Once again he found himself adopting a pseudonym to make contact with people he found utterly loathsome; and once again he scrupulously avoided using untruths.

He wrote to the box number and told LGYM that he could give them some very interesting information about the private life of Charles Oxley! For security reasons he preferred to give the information directly to a person at a private address rather than through a box number. They rose to the bait, saying they would be glad if he could 'dish up the dirt on the nasty little worm.' (The 'nasty ... worm' was understandable, but Charles thought 'little' was most insulting!) The letter was signed 'Terry' and used a couple of expressions that made it clear he was Scottish. Charles wrote back to say, quite truthfully, that he worked part-time at Hamilton College and really had genuine information, but the nature of the information was such that he could not risk sending it where it might be intercepted.

Unfortunately, the trail went cold at that point, as Charles was unable to bring the LGYM representatives out in the open. If he had been able to obtain names and addresses, Scotland Yard would certainly have brought charges.

Having tried often to influence the legislators at Westminster, Charles had the satisfaction of adding an amendment to some legislation on one occasion. It happened as a result of attending, in March 1986, the launch in London of the National Council for Christian Standards in Society. The Society published a magazine called *Moral Choice* and Charles contributed an article on child abuse to the first issue. He was elected to serve as Chairman of the Education Sub-committee, which met in early April. At that meeting he drafted an amendment to the Education Reform Act, which was going through the House of Lords at the time; Viscount Buckmaster, who was present at the meeting, agreed to propose the amendment during the debate. It laid on local authorities the duty to ensure that sex education must have regard to the moral implications and to the family. To the delight of many, including Charles, the amendment was carried, (although this particular battleground was still being contested fourteen years later).

In April 1986 Charles was invited, as Vice-President of the National Viewers and Listeners Association, to a weekend conference on 'The Media and the Police'. It was organised by the St Catharine's Foundation and took place in Cumberland Lodge, Windsor Great Park. Leading figures from the press and television met with senior police officers and other interested parties to hear addresses and join in discussions about the ways in which the two groups operate in relation to each other. The occasion is worthy of mention here because of what Charles wrote in his letter of thanks to the organiser: 'I have attended very many conferences over the past thirty-five years and have organised several during that time, but I have never enjoyed a conference so much as the one held on 4th to 6th April on "The Media and the Police".' An added bonus had been the opportunity to attend Matins in the Royal Chapel and to exchange a few words with Queen Elizabeth the Queen Mother.

In his capacity as Chairman of the Campaign for Law and Order he was often invited on to radio and television when topics such as capital punishment were under discussion. Charles accepted as many invitations as possible, so as to express the views of those Christians who advocate capital punishment. He did not know it at the time, but his opportunities to put the message across in this way were soon to be curtailed.

In August 1986 a visit to the doctor revealed that he had cancer in the prostate gland and that the disease had spread into the pelvic bones and lower spine. For a man who had enjoyed excellent health throughout his life this was a sudden and severe shock. He insisted that only the very minimum number of people should know about the cancer, including Muriel and their daughter Rachel who lived with them. Much later the three sons and other members of the family would be told, but in the meantime Charles intended to live as normally as possible. As it happened, the daughter of one of his Scarisbrick Hall teachers was a nurse at Wrightington Hospital in Lancashire and recognised him when he went there for implant surgery and blood transfusions. Even so, a large measure of confidentiality was maintained for several months, although his gradual loss of weight did elicit half-joking remarks at gatherings of the extended Oxley clan: 'Ee, Uncle Charlie's looking a bit peaky, Auntie Muriel—aren't you feeding him properly?'

By the time of Sports Days at the three schools in June 1987, some of the parents and visitors noticed that he was not his usual sprightly self and certainly seemed thinner in the face. Questions were asked, but answered as indirectly as possible.

In February of that year Charles had qualified for his British Rail Senior Citizen Railcard, but neither his sixty-five years nor his illness would stop him from carrying out his busy schedule. Indeed, he was so busy that he was having to apologise to one group or another when appointments clashed. He wrote a letter of apology for having missed an executive committee meeting of the National Council for Christian Standards in Society, concluding with the admission '... I am beginning to realise that I have taken on more than I can really cope with.'

A glance at his diary for 1987 shows just how demanding his commitments were. The week of January 19th to 25th, for example, included the following:—

Monday	9.00am	TV Channel 4 Debate on Law and Order
	11.30am	New Scotland Yard re LGYM
	12.30pm	Home Office
	2.15pm	DES re Hodder & Stoughton English book
Tuesday		Tower and Scarisbrick
Wednesday		Hamilton
Thursday	12.45pm	NCCSS Businessmen's promotion—London buffet lunch and 5 minute talk
	8.00pm	Crosby: Merseyside Independent Schools Action Committee

Friday	9.30am	Tower College Entrance Test
		BBC Manchester re James Anderton
Saturday	10.00am	Tower College Showround
	2.00pm	Liverpool City Mission Preachers' Seminar
Sunday	12.30 for 1.00pm	Paddington Hotel: Prof. Cox—'Crises in Education'

Three visits to London, two to Liverpool, one to Manchester, one to Hamilton, interspersed with 'normal' events at Tower College and Scarisbrick Hall School.

If Mary Whitehouse was unable to accept an invitation to speak for NVALA, she would often pass it on to Charles. That was how he came to be travelling to Gordonstoun School in the north-east of Scotland in March 1987 to address two hundred Sixth Form students and some senior staff. He set off from Tower at 7.30 in the morning with Dennis Wood, the Scarisbrick Hall caretaker, as his co-driver. After fitting in an hour at Hamilton College, he continued up to the coast of Morayshire, reaching Gordonstoun at 4 p.m., ready for the lecture at 5 o'clock. He addressed the gathering for thirty-five minutes and, such was the response from the students, the normal twenty-five minutes of questions was extended to forty-five minutes—an all-time record, according to the Head of Sixth Form.

Gordonstoun had offered overnight accommodation as well as generous travelling expenses, but Charles preferred to be on his way home, knowing that there was a showround of prospective parents at Scarisbrick Hall the following morning. He and his co-driver set off from Elgin at 6.40 p.m. and reached Tower at 2 a.m. Why spend so much time, effort and petrol for a meeting that lasted eighty minutes? To ask the question is to show a lack of understanding of what made Charles Oxley the man he was. He would not want to miss any opportunity to sow seeds in alert, young minds, particularly as some of those who heard him would go on to become leaders in different walks of life.

A sticker in the rear window of Charles' car proclaimed, as unequivocally as its owner might have done: 'ABORTION KILLS BABIES'. On a previous car, the message was not as blunt, but equally challenging: 'If abortion had been legal then, would you have been here now?' He regarded the Abortion Act of 1967 as one of the most disreputable pieces of legislation ever enacted by Parliament; it epitomised Roy (now Lord) Jenkins' tenure at the Home Office and the flood of permissiveness that swept away much Christian morality in the sixties and seventies. Now that scans and other scientific developments have enabled us to catch up with the Bible's description of fully formed human beings growing in their mother's womb, the deliberate killing of more than three million unborn babies since 1967 compares in horror with the Nazi holocaust.

Charles' revulsion at the slaughter led him to become a life member of the Society for the Protection of the Unborn Child. He also chaired a debate in the assembly hall at Hamilton College one Sunday evening on the merits of the Abortion Law. Religious journalist and broadcaster Stewart Lamont and Rev. Helen Johnston, a minister and hospital chaplain from Dundee, argued that the law should stay more or less as it was. Those putting the case for a tightening of the law were Rev. Dr Nigel Cameron, Warden of Rutherford House, Edinburgh, and Sarah Brown, a full-time pro-life worker and secretary of the Human Life Council. More than four hundred people attended the debate; the motion 'that the present abortion law should be reviewed by the government' was overwhelmingly approved. The audience were able to address questions to the main speakers and Charles had to ensure a fair hearing for both sides. It was agreed that the outcome of the debate should be passed on to the Prime Minister and to the Hamilton MP, George Robertson.

Throughout the first half of 1987 Charles continued to accept speaking appointments with churches and other groups. In April, for example, he spoke to the Glasgow Christian Businessmen's meeting on 'Christian Values in Society'. On a rather different tack he addressed the midweek meeting of the Bethany assembly in Haydock, St Helens, on 'Heresies', listing and explaining a total of thirteen, from Docetism to Apollinarianism to Monophysitism!

The cancer in his body did nothing to stifle the crusader in his spirit. At a Conservative constituency meeting addressed by Edwina Currie MP, the three hundred or so party supporters broke out in cheering when Charles addressed six questions to the Junior Health Minister:—

Why does the Government encourage indiscipline in schools by banning corporal punishment?

Why does the Government persistently refuse to proscribe paedophile organisations?

Why does the Government permit blasphemy and obscenity on television by refusing to extend the application of the Obscene Publications Act to broadcasting?

Why does the Government grant legal and social acceptance of sodomy in certain circumstances?

Why does the Government refuse a binding referendum on capital punishment for murder?

And, worst of all, WHY DOES THE GOVERNMENT REFUSE TO DO ANYTHING ABOUT THE NATIONAL SCANDAL OF ABORTION?

These of course were some of the issues on which he had spent a lifetime campaigning, urging those in authority to return to the Judaeo-Christian values which had made British democracy and culture the envy of the world. Mrs Currie's feeble attempts to answer only three of Charles' questions satisfied neither him nor the other people present, so he wrote to Norman (now Lord) Tebbit, the Conservative Party Chairman, deploring the fact that politicians' pronouncements on moral issues never actually led to changes in legislation.

By August 1987 the visits to Wrightington Hospital were becoming more frequent, the appointments in the diary were thinning out and the once-meticulous handwriting began to waver. Bookings previously accepted now had to be cancelled, for although his spirit remained ever willing, the energy was being eroded by the cancer.

After the school summer holidays, staff at the three schools saw a marked difference in Charles' appearance; and his voice, which for such a big man had always been surprisingly gentle, became husky and tired. He withdrew largely from visible involvement in the daily routines of the schools but remained busy behind the scenes, preparing for the future and calmly setting things in order.

Three dates stood out in his diary for October: Speech Day and Prizegiving at each of the schools. What would normally have been like gentle strolls in the foothills became testing peaks to be overcome only with pain and effort. Thursday 1st October: Scarisbrick Hall ...

Thursday 8th October: Hamilton College ... the original Tower College date on the 15th had to be postponed to the 22nd. Nobody present at any of the three occasions could doubt that they had seen a very sick and a very courageous man, most of them for the last time.

The day after the Tower Speech Day, Charles sent out a letter to all parents and members of staff explaining the nature of his illness and the arrangements he had made for the future of the schools. He had formed a separate company to run Hamilton College and he would be Chairman of the Board of Governors, with Muriel and Rachel also on the Board, along with three eminent Scotsmen who fully shared the Oxley educational philosophy and aims. The Assistant Principal of the College, Stuart Mitchell, had been appointed Principal in place of Charles, who would thus be relieved of the routine work of the College and the six-hour round trips at least once a week.

Charles continued to deal with correspondence and administrative matters at Tower and Scarisbrick for as long as possible, and when he was no longer able to carry out these functions, Muriel assumed full responsibility as Principal, to add to her already considerable commitment to the schools.

The final sentence of Charles' letter to parents and staff drew admiration from many: 'I am thankful for having had 64 years of perfect health and I face the future calmly with a firm faith in my Lord and Saviour, Jesus Christ.'

On Monday morning, 9th November 1987, a telephone call came through to my office at Scarisbrick Hall, from Tower College. It was Muriel Oxley, asking me to drive across there as her husband had some things he wanted to say to me. I had been on the staff of Scarisbrick Hall School for nineteen years, of which five were as deputy head and ten as headmaster. I had been told about the cancer from the time when it was diagnosed, but having observed the deterioration in the great man's condition I knew it would not be an easy conversation. On arrival at Tower I was led up to his bedroom by Muriel.

He lay propped up on the pillows, every breath a battle, every movement a torture, yet his spirit and sense of humour shone through indomitably. Whenever his speech slurred a little, Muriel prompted, knowing his mind. He handed me two typed A4 sheets of instructions about his funeral, to be conducted by Bertie Bullock, the husband of Muriel's niece, and about a memorial service which was to be my responsibility. He insisted on two elements in both services: firstly, that the hymns should be sung joyfully and 'with gusto ... nothing morbid'; and secondly, that the gospel message of salvation through faith in Jesus Christ should be clearly proclaimed. He wanted his own death to provide an opportunity for eternal life for others. Before I left, I was able to thank him for all that I had learnt from his example and to congratulate him for having fought the good fight so faithfully for his Lord.

When the telephone rang before breakfast at my home the following Monday, it was Muriel to let me know that her husband had passed away peacefully the night before.

It was standing room only for the large crowd who attended the funeral service in St Helens; among the police controlling traffic outside the parish church in Rainhill for the interment was a former pupil of Scarisbrick Hall. Billy Strachan, the Principal of Capernwray Hall Bible College, led the graveside service with his customary touches of humour, while Muriel maintained remarkable dignity and determination as, dry-eyed, she gave a strong lead in the hymn-singing.

'I don't grieve for my husband,' she said, 'because he has gone to be with the Lord, which is far better. Grief and tears would be rather selfish, expressing our sense of loss, when really what we want to emphasise is gratitude for his life and achievements.'

These sentiments also came to the fore in the memorial service held a few weeks later at the Floral Hall, Southport, the scene of many Scarisbrick Hall Speech Days. Pupils, staff and parents of Tower and Scarisbrick came together to remember with thankfulness what Charles Oxley had achieved, not only in establishing three fine schools but also in the moral crusades which led him into public life.

In accordance with Charles' wishes, a clear gospel message was proclaimed with conviction by John Sutton-Smith, Scarisbrick's deputy head, and it is known that at least four people made a commitment of their lives to Jesus Christ at the end of the service. And the hymn-singing? Once again, Muriel gave a strong lead to the twelve hundred people present, and Charles' choice of hymns provided every opportunity for the lively singing he wanted: 'Lift up your hearts! We lift them, Lord, to Thee'; 'We rest on Thee, our Shield and our Defender'; and 'Thine be the glory, risen, conquering Son'.

The newspaper obituaries paid suitable tribute, especially for his moral campaigning. *The Daily Telegraph* described him as 'a private school master of the strictest moral convictions and an indefatigable campaigner against pornography.' The *Liverpool Echo* quoted Mary Whitehouse: 'I am deeply grieved at his death because he was a man of such immense courage. He showed a simple, uncomplicated commitment to the things he believed to be right and true.' The same paper, in its leader column, expressed the view that 'every parent owes a debt to Charles Oxley, the Merseyside law and order campaigner ... Mr Oxley was uncompromising in his views, some of which were considered extreme even by those who agreed with him on other matters. But he did more than most of us to expose evil and to cause us to think about the direction in which society is moving.'

Another newspaper headline referred to him as 'The Gentle Giant who broke child sex group' and Joe Riley's piece in the *Liverpool Daily Post* was headed 'Quiet man with the roar of a lion': '... In many ways, he was his own best publicist: when journalists were not asking his views, he was busy writing letters to editors. To many people he was an enigma. Meet him casually, and he spoke in almost hushed tones. He was gentlemanly to a fault. But Charles Oxley was also about fire and brimstone.'

After summarising the campaigns in which Charles was active, Riley added: 'Certainly, he will be remembered and spoken of as long as the issues in which he so vehemently believed are debated. For over the years, for better or for worse, he has taken part in society as a national as well as a local figure.'

§

THE LASTING IMPRESSION of Charles Oxley has many facets. The public persona in no way typified the man. Those who would think of him as a strident, aggressive advocate of the death penalty and the birch did not know the quietly-spoken scholar or the fun-loving father and grandfather.

He hated sitting still, if still meant inactive. Even in the barber's chair having his short-back-and-sides, he would be composing the draft of a letter or making notes for a speech or an article. Sleep and mealtimes were necessary but regrettable intrusions into matters of greater importance; one reason why he hated Christmas Day and Boxing Day was that he could not legitimately be at work in his study. There were always books to be read and articles to be written, ideas to be generated and plans to be developed.

He wrote a tract entitled *4 Minutes Warning!* in which he highlighted the time we would each have had to prepare for a nuclear attack when the alarm sounded. Posing the question: How *do* you prepare for death?, he then gave the Christian answer with appropriate verses of Scripture.

He even wrote a 'psalm', prompted by the experience of trying to pass weekend drivers one frustrating Bank Holiday Monday:—

Behold, the sun riseth in the heavens
    and shineth forth in all his glory.
For today the marketplace shall remain silent
    and they who lend silver upon us shall cease.
Then doth the stranger venture into the highway
    and the unstable doth get in the way of the speedy.
The fool looketh neither to the right hand nor to the left,
    yea, he wandereth whithersoever he will:
He meditates upon the splendour of the heavens
    and rejoices with them that go with him on the way.
Sudden destruction shall overtake him,
    yet knoweth he not the cause thereof:
Even he that is steadfast shall be overthrown,
    yea, he shall be cast into the ditch.
Then shall the keepers of the highway descend upon them
    and charge the innocent with folly.
They that sit in judgement shall declare him guilty
    and he that causeth the calamity shall laugh.
The wise man sitteth in his own house;
    yea, he abideth securely in his own dwelling.

The 'Needed Truth' assemblies of the Brethren movement published an illustrated monthly magazine for young people, and between March and September 1955, Charles contributed a series on the Seven Wonders of the Ancient World. Each one had a detailed drawing with Charles' graphic description, leading to some point of Christian challenge to the young readers. Nowadays the articles would appear quaint and old-fashioned, but to children unused to commercialism, television or pop culture, they would be a delight.

Any teacher enjoys the 'howlers' the pupils come up with and Charles was no exception; he wrote some of them down in a notebook he entitled *Pupils' Picturesque Poppycock*. Some of the Bible story versions are worthy of Mrs Malaprop herself: 'Solomon presided at the desecration of the temple'; 'Moses' mother put him in a basket and pitched it outside'; 'After the flood, the ark rested on Mount Anorak'; 'the sin of the Pharisees was that they did things at the street corners which other people did in the closets'!

Having set up three successful independent schools, Charles received numerous invitations to take over established schools or set up more new ones. The theory was admirable: not only could he campaign against the decline of educational and moral standards, but he could also run a chain of Christian schools all round the country to promote high standards of achievement and morality. His support for such endeavours in India underlines the seriousness with which he took these responsibilities. Nevertheless, although he visited several properties to view their potential, the only additional one he actually purchased was destined not to become a school after all.

Halkyn Castle had once been the country residence of the Duke of Westminster, who invited friends to stay there when they came north for the Chester race meetings. Latterly, it had been owned by a Colonel Bevan, from whom Charles and Muriel bought it in 1978 for £45,000. The modernised A55 road speeds the holidaymakers along the North Wales coast to Colwyn Bay, Llandudno and Anglesey, but a turn inland, up the hill, leads to the little village of Halkyn with the castle set back in the trees behind the village. From the castle grounds, echoing to the sound of peacocks in the courtyard, the view sweeps down across the Dee estuary and Welsh coastline.

Although Charles and Muriel could visualise the castle as a school, the local council could not, and the whole project became so tangled up in red tape that they scrapped the idea. They considered other uses for the property, including an outdoor pursuits centre for young people, but in the end it remained a pleasant country retreat, visited occasionally by parties from Tower College or church groups.

Charles in cheerful mood.

Charles' financial generosity extended to many worthy causes and individual needs. When a new Brethren assembly began in Haydock, on the outskirts of St Helens, he made a loan of £12,000 available, interest-free, so that the small band of Christians could build their own meeting-hall. To another assembly he gave both a sizeable gift and another interest-free loan, so that they could set up a Christian work in Kirkby, one of the more troubled areas around Liverpool at that time. In Toxteth he gave money and encouragement to a group of Christians who came together in the aftermath of the riots.

Dianne Core, the founder of Childwatch, remembers how Charles came to her aid when she was running a group called Southport Women's and Children's Aid. She needed a safe lodging for some battered wives and when Charles heard about the need, he made boarding accommodation available at Scarisbrick Hall. Sanctuary of a different kind was provided by the Scarisbrick Hall lake, which became the permanent home of a pair of swans after Charles heard on the radio of the need for a safe haven for birds which had been injured.

In June 1985 Charles' war-time experience in the fire service came in useful. He was driving down the M6 in Cheshire when an accident caused a van to catch fire. Pulling in to the hard shoulder, he ran to help the driver until the police and fire brigade arrived. He later received a letter of thanks from the Motorway Unit of Cheshire Constabulary, praising his actions and thanking him for his 'valuable assistance'.

Charles' care for individuals can be seen in the help he gave to an old friend, Laurence Porter; this schoolmaster and Bible scholar had had both legs amputated, so Charles made it his responsibility to take Laurence to the annual Swanwick Conference of Brethren and to look after him. That was no straightforward task, as it meant lifting him from car to wheelchair, from wheelchair to bathroom, from bathroom to bed, and doing all he could to make the weekend as enjoyable as possible for his friend. And all this at a time when, as a convenor of the Conference, Charles had certain organisational responsibilities for the weekend.

Menial tasks were never a problem for him, even though he was such a big man with a commanding presence. Not long after I joined the staff of Scarisbrick Hall School in 1968, I went out to my car at the end of a school day to find that the exhaust pipe had broken apart, causing a noise like a tank. I went back into the Hall to find a boarding boy who could help me, but the first person I met was Charles himself. When he heard what my problem was he insisted on helping me, crawling under the car in his smart suit to hold the two ends of the pipe together while I effected a temporary repair.

Such was his massive workload that it is hard to imagine him relaxing, yet he could be the life and soul of the party when he did take time off for leisure. One sunny Saturday we took some of the Scarisbrick boarders to Halkyn Castle for a day out. These were youngsters who had helped out serving tea at parents' evenings or those whose guardians rarely came to take them out for the weekend. For the Oxleys, of course, leisure simply meant a break from routine, not an absence of work. Charles, Muriel and Rachel did all the work themselves: a conducted tour of the castle and grounds; serving a magnificent cooked lunch fit for royalty; at tea-time laying out and serving an equally sumptuous picnic on the lawn; and doing all the washing-up afterwards, despite others volunteering to help. In between times, Charles removed his tie—amazingly—to join in a game of cricket with the boys, then had all the children yelling delightedly in his wake as he charged round the garden with a large tin of Quality Street, throwing the contents high in the air for the chasing children to catch.

He had a keen sense of humour, enjoying sharing the latest funny story with anyone who would listen. Some of his scholarly Christian associates might have been surprised at one of his favourites: 'A scrap metal merchant died and duly arrived at the pearly gates, where he was met by a rather dubious St Peter. "Scrap metal merchant, eh?" queried Peter. "I don't think we've had one of those before; I'd better go off and check." Off he went, and when he came back, the man had disappeared and so had the pearly gates!'

His humour and generosity combined beautifully in an incident in 1981. John Sutton-Smith, deputy head at Scarisbrick Hall, was in charge of examination entries and had omitted to include the entry of a girl for an 'A' Level re-sit. When he realised, he submitted a 'late entry form' and paid the additional £15 out of his own pocket as it had been his mistake. A little while later he found on the staff-room letter rack an envelope addressed to him in Charles Oxley's familiar handwriting. Inside he found a note:—

> 'Tis verily a grievous wrong
> You've been an' gorn an' did;
> But you've confessed and I forgive,
> So here's the fifteen quid.
>
> C.A.O.

Bible texts on railway station hoardings appear there because of the generosity of people like Charles Oxley. Runcorn station is on the main line from Liverpool to London, very busy with inter-city passengers who alight there in preference to using the centre of Liverpool. Nearby Widnes is a major centre of the chemical industry and senior personnel from ICI use Runcorn station every day. 'Where better to place a Bible text?' thought Charles on one of his journeys to London, so he contacted the Bible Text Publicity Mission and sent the requisite amount to put up a text. They regularly receive letters from grateful travellers who have been challenged or comforted by the sight of a Bible verse at a station.

Though few Christian standard-bearers would ever fight in quite the same way as Charles, he recognised the valuable contribution made by those with a similar agenda. Mrs Victoria Gillick fought against the provision of contraceptives for teenage girls without their parents' knowledge and she recalled speaking at a public meeting in St Helens where Charles was the chairman.

> I do remember how I was struck by his own gentleness and humour and humility. I found it hard to believe that this was the man who had had such enormous courage as to tackle the insidious perverts of P I E. His self-effacing manner belied the bravery of the man.
>
> He was also a generous and thoughtful man when it came to helping me, after the Law Lords finally ruled against me. Within a few days of that judgement, Mr Oxley had written words of encouragement and sent me £20 for the 'fighting fund', for both of which I was truly grateful.

When the controversy over the film *The Life of Brian* was at its height and Charles' views made the front-page headlines in the *St Helens Reporter*, one lady wrote critically about him and provoked a response from another, whose letter included the following words, a suitable tribute to a remarkable man:—

> Has this lady met Charles Oxley to assume his fear of the Christian Church being threatened by the showing of this film? Not so. I have met him quite a few times and he is not a man to speak before thinking.
>
> He also knows the strength of the foundations of Christianity in the world today. His work as a headmaster and principal involves children and teenagers. He knows how the minds of the young work and he is concerned about them and their future lives. The children of today are the adults of tomorrow.
>
> A greater Christian I have yet to meet.